Mysteries of the Universe

ABOVE *The Loch Ness monster, photographed in May 1977.*
OVERLEAF *The pyramid of Chephren at dawn.*
CONTENTS PAGES *Stone circle at Callanish, island of Lewis.*
ENDPAPERS *The Orion nebula, a glowing cloud of gas with four new-born stars at its centre.*

MYSTERIES OF THE UNIVERSE

Richard Cavendish

Galahad Books

First published in the United States of America in 1981 by Galahad Books
95 Madison Avenue
New York, New York 10016
By arrangement with George Weidenfeld & Nicolson Ltd, London

Library of Congress Catalog Card Number: 81–81152
ISBN: 0–88365–559–4

Printed in Italy

Contents

Lost Worlds

Lost Worlds

Mysteries are fascinating because they suggest that reality is richer and stranger than the conventional wisdom admits. Yet by definition a mystery has no satisfactory explanation in the present state of knowledge, and so a book about mysteries is bound to ask far more questions than it can answer.

Did the Egyptian pyramids and the stone circles of prehistoric Europe enshrine a secret wisdom? Does a grid of invisible lines of power stretch across the earth, understood and harnessed by our ancestors long ago? Is a photograph of Jesus Christ preserved on a faded strip of cloth in Turin Cathedral? Are some places, like Stonehenge or Glastonbury or Lourdes, charged with an unexplained force? Are there warps or loops in time? Is there a fifth dimension, into which people and things sometimes disappear, and from which they may or may not reappear? Has the earth been visited by beings from outer space? Are dinosaurs still alive? Has Neanderthal man survived for thousands of years in remote corners of the globe?

If there were clear-cut answers to these questions, and many others like them, they would not be mysteries. The evidence on which to base an answer is usually inadequate, fragmentary and uncertain. It frequently depends on eyewitness accounts of things seen or experienced, and eyewitness accounts are notoriously difficult to assess. The line between fact and fantasy is hard, and often impossible, to draw. Because the evidence is inadequate, mysteries tend to have a bewildering variety of tentative explanations, which adds to the confusion.

People's attitudes to mysteries are based far more on temperament than on evidence. At one end of the scale are the temperamentally credulous, determined to believe six improbable things before breakfast, and the more improbable the better. At the other are the temperamentally sceptical, equally determined not to believe, and committed to the unlikely assumption that we already know everything of importance there is to know about ourselves and the world around us. No previous generation could correctly have made this assumption and there is no good reason for thinking that we can. Nor is the sceptics' appeal to reason and scientific method as convincing as it should be, because so many advances in knowledge have been made in the teeth of entrenched opposition from scientists and the 'reasonable' orthodoxy of the day.

If there are important areas of reality still to be discovered, then no doubt there are already indications of them. The difficulty is to decide which of the indications are genuinely promising and which are mares' nests. All we can do is to hold as firmly as possible to common sense – while remembering that the world is certainly a much odder place than we were brought up to think.

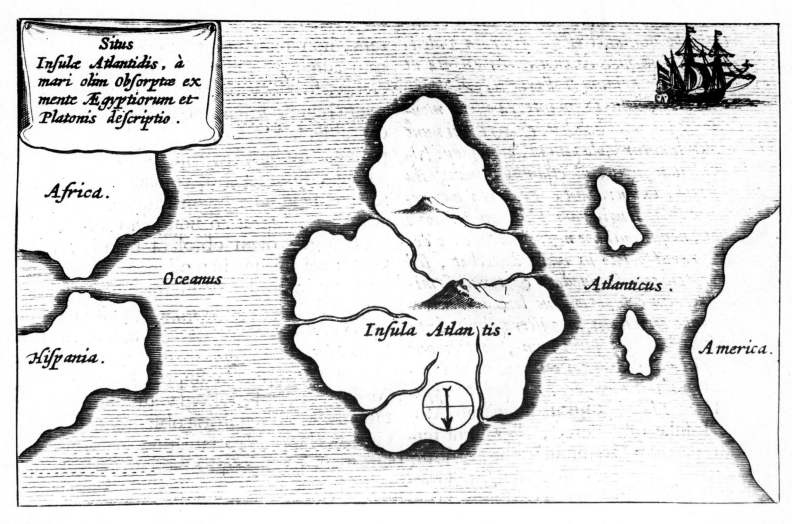

The Destruction of Atlantis

Among the most enticing mysteries that fascinate modern writers and readers are those of the 'lost civilizations' of Atlantis and Lemuria. The idea of a lost paradise which might be rediscovered, a place of idyllic happiness, supreme wisdom, fabulous wealth and power, has long haunted the human imagina-

ABOVE *This seventeenth-century map shows the island of Atlantis in the middle of the Atlantic between Africa and Spain on one side and America on the other. South is at the top, in contrast to modern maps. From* Mundus Subterraneus *by Athanasius Kircher.*

OPPOSITE The Garden of Eden *by Rubens and Brueghel. In the Middle Ages it was believed that the idyllic paradise where Adam and Eve lived peacefully with the animals at the beginning of history still existed somewhere on earth and might one day be rediscovered.*

PREVIOUS PAGES *Mount Shasta stands in a remote region of northern California. Every now and again fanciful stories and rumours go the rounds about a community of white-robed Lemurians who live on the mountain, using gold nuggets for currency and worshipping in a great Mayan-style temple.*

tion. In medieval times it was believed that the Garden of Eden, where Adam and Eve lived peacefully and contentedly at the dawn of history, still existed on earth, somewhere just beyond the borders of known geography. The kingdom of Prester John, a utopia of unimaginable riches and marvellous inventions, was believed to be somewhere in the East, perhaps in India or in the mysterious mountain–fastnesses of Ethiopia. There are old Celtic legends of magic islands of immortality across the sea to the west, one of them being Avalon, the paradise of apple trees, to which the wounded King Arthur was taken after his last battle. After the discovery of the Americas in the late fifteenth century stories circulated in Europe of cities fabulously rich in gold, and expeditions were mounted to search for them; but nothing meeting the explorers' eager expectations was ever discovered.

Atlantis belongs to the same pattern of ideas, and some writers describe it as the first home of the human race and the cradle of civilization. The original story comes from Plato, in two of his books (*Timaeus* and *Critias*). According to Plato, the famous Athenian statesman

Solon visited Egypt and was told by the Egyptian priests that, nine thousand years before, there had been a powerful empire in the Atlantic ruled from the island of Atlantis, which lay opposite the Straits of Gibraltar. Atlantis was rich in gold and silver, and the Atlanteans were great architects and engineers. They built magnificent temples and palaces, harbours and docks, canals and bridges. For many generations they were a wise and virtuous people, law-abiding and civilized; but they were corrupted by power and wealth. They massed an army against Greece and Egypt, and Zeus, the supreme god, determined to destroy them. There were violent earthquakes and floods, and in a day and night Atlantis sank beneath the sea.

Solon lived about 600 BC and, adding on Plato's nine thousand years, Atlantis must have been destroyed about 9600 BC, far earlier than any such advanced civilization is believed to have existed. Aristotle, who was Plato's pupil, thought Plato made the whole story up in order to illustrate his political theories. On the other hand, much of Plato's description of Atlantis resembles the civilization of Crete in the Bronze

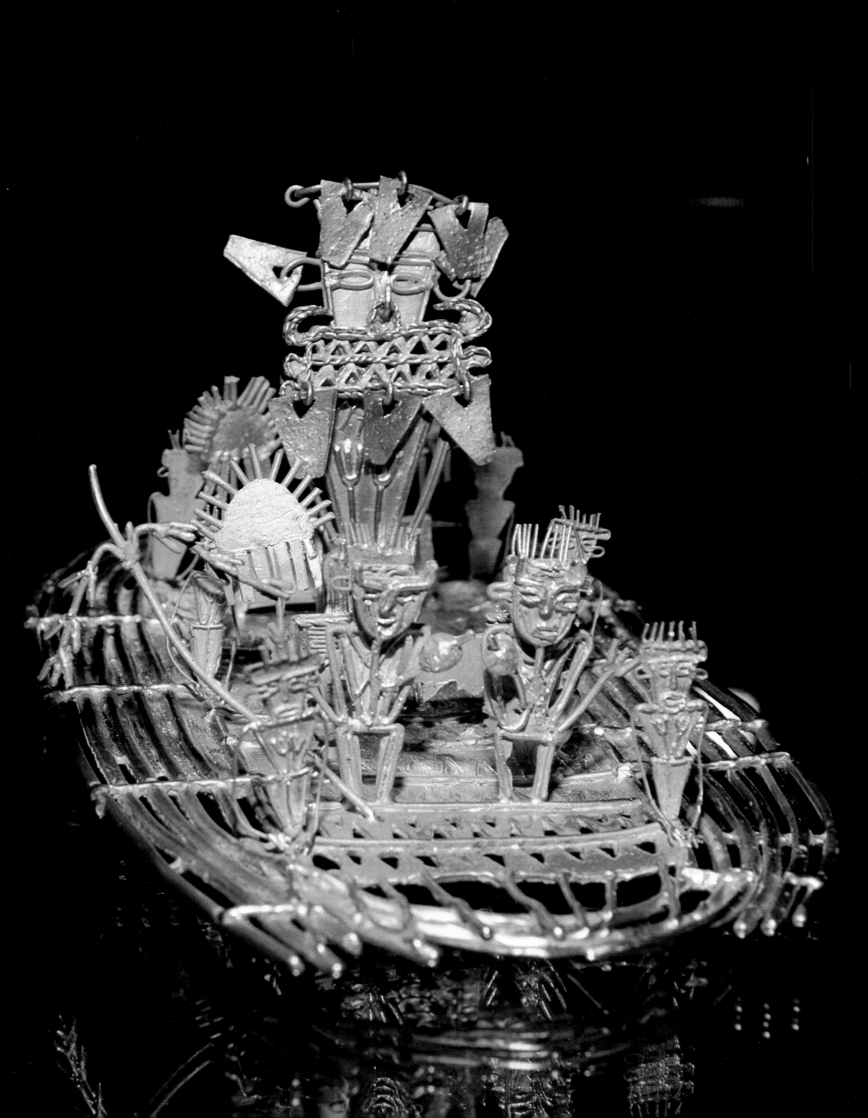

Age, when it was a formidable sea power. It is known that a gigantic volcanic explosion occurred at the island of Thera (or Santorini), not far north of Crete, in about 1500 BC. The centre of Thera disappeared under water; it is thought that Crete itself was seriously affected and that this accounts for the sudden decline of Cretan power. Perhaps it is a distant memory of this catastrophe which lies behind Plato's story of the island sinking beneath the sea and the sudden destruction of a civilization. If the figure of nine thousand years was a mistake for nine hundred years, the date would be 1500 BC, which is about right for the Thera explosion.

This is the most promising theory yet advanced to account for the legend of Atlantis, but it has its difficulties. Whether the Thera explosion did in fact cause the sudden collapse of Cretan civilization is doubtful, and are we justified in arbitrarily knocking a nought off Plato's nine thousand years? What Plato says suggests that the Egyptian priests were talking about a period further back in the past than 1500 BC, and Plato puts Atlantis firmly in the Atlantic, not in the eastern Mediterranean.

OPPOSITE *After the conquest of Peru by the Spaniards, stories began to circulate about El Dorado, 'the golden man', said to be the chief of a tribe fabulously rich in gold. In a special ritual he would take a raft out on to a lake and throw golden objects into the water as sacrifices.*

RIGHT AND ABOVE *Plato's description of the civilization of Atlantis has much in common with Bronze Age Crete, whose kings ruled a maritime empire from their palace at Knossos. The complexity of the palace buildings, now ruined, may have sparked off the legend of the Cretan labyrinth, in which lurked a monster, the Minotaur.*

The Search for Atlantis

Speculation about Atlantis continued all through the Middle Ages and was given a fresh impetus by the discovery of America. Authors from Sir Francis Bacon in the seventeenth century to the German naturalist von Humboldt in the nineteenth identified Atlantis with the American continent itself. It was suggested that Plato had heard rumours of the Americas, which had possibly been discovered by adventurous Phoenician seamen. Innumerable other locations, from Portugal to Sri Lanka, and from the Arctic, Greenland or Siberia to South Africa have been claimed as the site of the vanished Atlantis by one enthusiast or another. In 1953 it was announced that the ruins of the Atlantean citadel had been seen by North Sea divers, off Heligoland.

The main line of speculation, however, puts Atlantis where Plato said it was, in the Atlantic. If the Atlantic were drained, a long mountainous ridge would be visible, running north-south from Iceland to the Antarctic. This ridge is often claimed as the backbone of the sunken Atlantis, overwhelmed by the melting of the glaciers at the end of the last Ice Age, about twelve thousand years ago; but geologists dismiss this as nonsense.

An alternative theory is that Atlantis was where the West Indian islands are now, and that it was inundated by the sea about 3500 BC. In 1968 lines of rectangular stones were discovered under water off Bimini in the Bahamas, and were thought to be the remains of a road or causeway constructed by the Atlanteans. Whether the supposed causeway is really man-made, however, is in considerable doubt. In 1979 Russian oceanographers reported that they had seen massive walls and stairways deep in the Atlantic, midway between Portugal and Madeira. They thought these were the ruins of Atlantis, but were promptly castigated by supporters of the Cretan theory.

All sorts of far-fetched speculations have clustered round Atlantis. The Atlanteans are said to have colonized the Mediterranean, the western coasts of Europe, the shores of the Baltic, the Black Sea and the Caspian, the Mississippi River, the Amazon and the South American coasts. They founded civilization and it was their wisdom and technical skill that inspired the building of the Egyptian pyramids and the great prehistoric monuments of Europe, such as Stonehenge. The story of the Garden of Eden conceals the memory of Atlantis and its fall. The kings and queens of Atlantis became the gods and goddesses of the ancient world, and Olympus and Asgard, the homes of the Greek and Norse gods, were originally Atlantis. Some writers credit the Atlanteans with the invention of flying machines, television, explosives, and lasers. It is even said that their lasers, now sunk deep in the western Atlantic, are responsible for the disappearances of ships and aircraft in the notorious Bermuda Triangle!

All this rests not on evidence but on the wistful longing for a lost paradise. The Atlantis of modern imagining combines high civilization and advanced technology with wisdom, happiness, and peace. It is precisely this combination which eludes modern man, and which gives the legendary Atlantis its magnetic allure.

Lemuria, Mu and Shambhala

The same is true of Atlantis's less well-known cousin in the Indian Ocean (or the Pacific). The theory that a vanished continent once existed between Madagascar and Malaya was put forward by scientists in the nineteenth century to account for similarities between animals, plant life and geology in areas separated by thousands of miles of sea. The hypothetical continent was christened Lemuria, from the lemur, which lives in Africa, southern India and

OPPOSITE *Plato wrote of the richly adorned royal palace of Atlantis, 'a marvel to behold for size and beauty'. Was he describing the sumptuous Minoan palace on Crete?*

BELOW *A still from the 1973 film version of James Hilton's best-selling novel* Lost Horizon, *in which two flyers discover a 'lost world' in the Himalayas in Tibet, an idyllic haven of ageless wisdom and perfect peace. Many readers believed that the story was founded on fact.*

Malaya. The German biologist Ernst Haeckel suggested that Lemuria was probably the cradle of the human race, which there emerged from the apes.

Occultists were attracted to this idea and decided that Lemuria had extended across the Pacific, the South Sea islands being all that was left of it. An army officer named James Churchward claimed to have discovered ancient stone tablets, hidden in a Hindu temple in India, which showed that the name of the Pacific continent was Mu. It was the original Garden of Eden, where human beings first developed and built up an advanced civilization. Colonists went out from Mu to all corners of the globe and the various races of mankind were descended from them. Mu was finally destroyed in a colossal volcanic cataclysm. But unfortunately no one else ever saw Colonel Churchward's tablets, and so they

cannot be taken seriously.

In 1933 James Hilton wrote a novel, *Lost Horizon*, in which two flyers lost in the Himalayas discover the ideal community of Shangri-La, cut off from the modern world, where time stands still and everyone lives in perfect tranquillity and wisdom. Many readers believed, and many still do, that the story was based on fact. There are numerous oriental traditions of a secret paradise of this kind, in Tibet or in the mountains of China, the Gobi Desert, or the Altai Mountains on the borders of Russia and Mongolia. One of its legendary names is Shambhala: 'quietude'. Similar rumours bob up to the surface now and again of a secret Lemurian monastery somewhere in the Andes in South America, or a secret Lemurian community on Mount Shasta in California. They are products of the deep human longing for a utopian haven of refuge.

Lost
Wisdom

Lost Wisdom

Most people in the West today have been brought up to believe that the record of the human race has been one of sustained progress; that the further back into the past you look, the more brutish, ignorant and stupid human beings must have been. The graph of civilization has been a steadily rising curve – allowing for minor fluctuations – which has reached its peak in the present century. It is confidently expected to go on rising in the future, unless of course we use our technology to destroy ourselves and the world with us.

This self-flattering viewpoint owes a good deal to the nineteenth-century theory of evolution through the survival of the fittest, with its implication that whatever is later in date must be 'fitter' than what went before. The results of recent research make it extremely difficult to go on accepting it. People very remote from us in time are now known to have possessed far more sophisticated knowledge and skill than archeologists and historians were ready to allow until quite recently.

At the same time, besides the evidence which is accumulating of the intellectual achievements of early man there is plenty pointing the other way. Thousands of years ago, massive stone monuments were built in Europe, the most famous being Stonehenge. Their design incorporates a remarkably advanced knowledge of astronomy and mathematics. The people of the time, however, lived by simple hunting and farming, inhabiting huts made of mud, wood and straw. In the earlier stages at least, they had no system of writing, no wheeled vehicles, no metal tools, only the simplest of equipment and the poorest of lives. And yet there were some of them whose scientific knowledge was far in advance of what most of us in the twentieth century possess, and who had the organizing ability to carry out projects which took hundreds of people and years of labour to complete.

How can these apparently opposite types of evidence be reconciled? The fact that we regard them as opposite says something about our own conventional outlook: we associate high intellectual achievement and civilization with industrial society and advanced technology. It looks as if this

assumption is wrong-headed. Also, it is likely that in early societies scientific and intellectual attainment was not common property, but was the preserve of elite groups which kept their knowledge and skill to themselves.

Did these elites know more than we recognize even now? Did they possess a rich store of wisdom, a true understanding of reality, which the world has lost? On the evidence we have it does not seem likely, but the evidence we have is only fragmentary. Modern man's experience demonstrates that wisdom and high scientific attainment do not necessarily go hand in hand. Early societies lived closer to nature than we do and were probably more at home with extra-sensory perception, the remarkable psychic faculties of the mind which twentieth-century science has begun to take seriously. In these ways at least they may have been wiser than ourselves.

Sirius, False Teeth and Electric Batteries

There are some startling examples of societies in many ways primitive and backward by modern standards, but rich in scientific knowledge. From about AD 200 to 900 the Mayan civilization in what is now southern Mexico and Guatemala was ruled by an elite skilled in astronomy, mathematics, geometry, architecture and sculpture. They had an accurate calendar, they could predict solar and lunar eclipses, and they calculated the cycles of the moon and the planets. The members of the elite lived in luxurious centres. The rest of the population were peasants, occupying wooden huts and grubbing a living from the soil.

In the late 1940s two French anthropologists went to study the Dogon people of West Africa, much of whose traditional culture has survived the impact of Christianity and Islam. The anthropologists discovered that the Dogon priests had an astonishing knowledge of the star Sirius, which played an important part in their religion. They knew that Sirius A, which is the brightest star in the sky, has a satellite, Sirius B, which revolves around it. Sirius B is invisible to the naked eye and the Dogon priests had no telescopes, but they knew that it exists and that its orbit round Sirius A is elliptical, not circular. They knew the position of Sirius A within the orbit and that the orbit takes fifty years. Sirius B was not discovered in the West by telescope until 1862 and was not photographed until 1970.

If, as seems to be the case, the Dogon priests' knowledge of astronomy is too old to be attributed to Western in-fluence, where did it come from? They themselves said that it came to their ancestors long ago from space-travellers, visitors from a planet attached to Sirius B who landed on earth. This seems extremely improbable. An alternative suggestion is that the Dogon learned their astronomy originally from Egypt and the Near East, where telescopes were probably in use in the distant past. Lenses made in about 2000 BC have been found in Crete and Asia Minor, and putting two lenses together to make a rudimentary telescope is a simple step.

ABOVE *The Soothsayer's Pyramid at Uxmal in Yucatan. The Mayan priesthood calculated the cycles of the moon and the planets.*

OPPOSITE *The civilizations of ancient Mexico were startlingly rich in astronomical and mathematical knowledge. The Pyramid of the Sun, Toltec, at San Juan Teotihuacan.*

PREVIOUS PAGES *The goddess Nephthys, from Tutankhamen's tomb.*

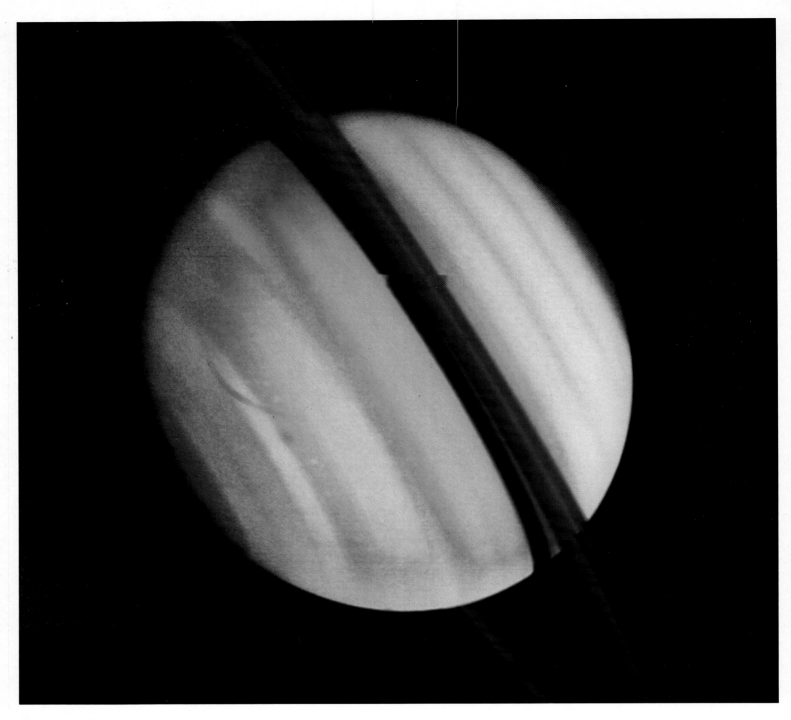

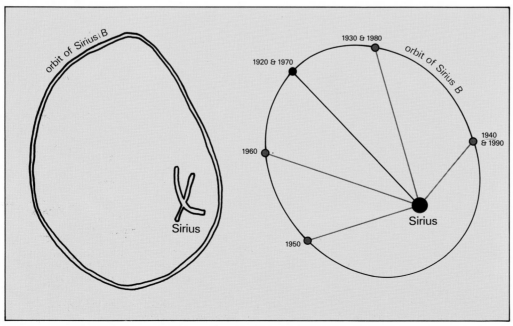

Dogon priests trace in the sand drawings that show a remarkable knowledge of astronomy. The rings of Saturn (above) are visible only through a powerful telescope, yet somehow the Dogon know the planet has a halo. Sirius B is a small star which describes an elliptical orbit around Sirius, as the Dogon drawing (far left) shows; but Sirius B is invisible to the naked eye, and was only discovered by the West in 1862.

However, whether anyone in the ancient Near East had a telescope which could see Sirius B is very much in doubt. Another explanation which has been suggested is that one or more Dogon priests centuries ago had psychic powers and gained their information by clairvoyance or 'far-seeing'. Modern research into extra-sensory perception has made this suggestion less patently ridiculous than it would have been fifty years ago, but it still seems distinctly far-fetched. Dogon astronomy remains a mystery.

High intelligence, organizational ability, and an advanced capacity for abstract thinking are evident in the pyramids of Egypt and the stone circles of prehistoric Europe, and in early human achievements in navigation, mining and metallurgy. The more that is discovered about these achievements, the earlier in date they turn out to be. Excavations on the Black Sea coast of Bulgaria have revealed the existence of a rich and technically highly skilled metal-working culture there in about 4500 BC, a much earlier date than would previously have been considered likely. More recently, copper mines dated to about 4000 BC have been found in Israel and in Spain.

The ancient Etruscans had false teeth, the Romans had central heating, the Egyptians used lightning conduc-

ABOVE Dogon dancers in Mali, West Africa. In the 1940s the priests of the Dogon people were discovered to possess a remarkably advanced knowledge of astronomy, which they said had been handed down to them from their ancestors, who learned it from visitors from space long ago.

BELOW An electric battery used for electroplating jewellery over seventeen centuries ago. This primitive cell – an iron rod in a copper cylinder – was dug up near Baghdad in 1936.

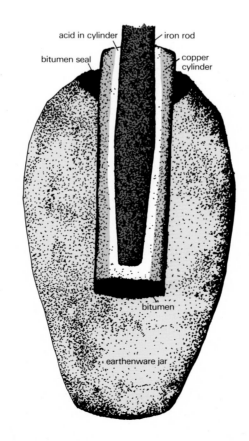

acid in cylinder / iron rod
bitumen seal / copper cylinder
bitumen
earthenware jar

tors, and part of a computer used for calculating astronomical positions, fished up by sponge-divers off a Greek island, has been dated to about 80 BC. Electric batteries were in use two thousand years ago. During excavations near Baghdad in Iraq in 1936 an object was found which proved to be a simple electric cell, dating from somewhere between the third century BC and the third AD. Others have been discovered and they are thought to have been used for electroplating gold and silver jewellery.

Exploitation of electricity may be much older and there is even a possibility, fantastic as it seems, that the builders of the Egyptian pyramids four thousand years ago used electric light. This is one way of explaining the puzzling fact that there are elaborate paintings deep inside the pyramids, on the walls of corridors that are pitch dark. How did the artists see to execute them? Torches or candles would have left black marks on the walls and ceilings, but there are no black marks. Perhaps battery-powered lights were used. Or perhaps the black marks were cleaned off, but could this have been done without leaving any trace? Or was a complicated system of mirrors and lenses used to bring daylight in from outside? Here again there is no certain answer.

The Egyptian Pyramids

Numerous other mysteries surround the Egyptian pyramids, especially the Great Pyramid at Giza, the largest and most spectacular of them all.

Ever since Greek and Roman times, the land of the Nile has enjoyed an awesome reputation for holding the key to lost secrets. The compelling glamour of ancient Egypt comes from the immense antiquity of its civilization, the splendour of its temples and monuments, its tombs with their sinister mummies, the strange animal-headed gods, the mysterious hieroglyphs or sacred writing, and the divine aura of the Egyptian pharaohs, who were believed to be gods on earth.

Greek and Roman writers credited the Egyptian priests with a mastery of powerful magic and a profound secret wisdom, symbolized by the Sphinx, the enigmatic figure which guards the pyramids of Giza. Arab writers in the early Middle Ages said that the pyramids were repositories of ancient Egyptian wisdom and scientific knowledge which the world had lost, and this idea was revived in the nineteenth

century with the first modern archeological investigations in Egypt.

The major period of pyramid-building in Egypt is known as the Old Kingdom (from roughly 2700 to 2200 BC) and the pyramids are believed to have been the royal tombs of the time. This is certainly borne out by the inscriptions found in some of the later ones, which include prayers and magic spells to give the dead king immortal life. The Egyptians thought it essential to preserve the physical body from decay if the soul was to live on after death. To achieve this they mummified the corpses of kings and other important and wealthy personages – the process was too expensive for ordinary people. The hot, porous sands of Egypt naturally disinfect and preserve corpses buried in them, which may have provided the impetus to the invention of more elaborate and efficient techniques.

According to the orthodox theory, the Old Kingdom pharaohs were buried inside colossal pyramids with complex interior passages and sealed chambers, partly to give them a resting-place in which they would be eternally undisturbed, and partly as a proud and lasting expression of the power and grandeur of Egypt.

The odd thing is, however, that no

bodies have ever been found in any of the pyramids. Sarcophagi (stone coffins) have been found, apparently intended for the dead kings, but always empty. The standard explanation is that grave-robbers broke in and stole the bodies, but this is not very convincing, especially as some of the empty sarcophagi seem not to have been opened or disturbed. Later pharaohs were buried in less grandiose tombs and when robbers broke in they stole the gold and jewels, but usually left the mummified bodies alone.

An alternative explanation is that the corridors and chambers which have been explored in the pyramids were blinds, meant to deceive robbers, and that the bodies were hidden in skilfully concealed compartments where they still lie undiscovered. Another is that after an epidemic of grave-robbing the priests opened up the burial chambers in the pyramids, took the bodies away, and concealed them in more modest tombs elsewhere.

There is no fully satisfactory explanation of this puzzle as yet. The Great Pyramid was built for King Cheops in the twenty-sixth century BC. The entrance was concealed in the north face of the pyramid, about 55 feet (17 m) above ground level. A narrow passage, only about 4 feet (1.2 m) high, led down to an ascending corridor, rising into the heart of the structure and giving access to the King's Chamber, as it is called: the apparent burial place of Cheops. Inside was a massive granite sarcophagus which must have been put there while the pyramid was still under construction, as it is too big to go through the ascending corridor.

In the ninth century AD the Caliph Mamun sent an expedition to explore the Great Pyramid. Failing to discover the original entrance, the party tunnelled into the pyramid lower down and came to the ascending corridor, which was blocked by three large granite plugs, tightly wedged in place. They tunnelled round the plugs, regained the ascending corridor on the far side and reached the King's Chamber. There was no sign of disturbance, but the sarcophagus was open and empty, and its lid was missing. What had happened to the body? One answer is that graverobbers stole it and the pyramid was later sealed up again – but it is difficult to see why, if the body was gone.

Rays and Razor Blades

Near the Great Pyramid stands the pyramid of Chephren, the successor of Cheops. It was first explored in modern times in 1818, but no trace of Chephren's body could be found. In 1968 Egyptian and American scientists X-rayed the pyramid, in the hope of detecting hitherto undiscovered chambers inside it. After more than a year they gave up, because their findings made no sense. Records made with the same equipment from the same point on successive days showed totally different ray-patterns. The head of the project called the results 'scientifically impossible' and said that 'there is some force that defies the laws of science at work in the pyramid'.

Other experiments suggest that there

ABOVE *The Egyptians went to enormous trouble and expense to preserve the bodies of the dead by mummifying them, so that the soul would live on. Modern experiments suggest that, for some unknown reason, the shape of the pyramid retards the decay of flesh and assists mummification.*

OPPOSITE *The enigmatic figure of the Sphinx sums up the air of magic and mystery which for thousands of years has surrounded the pyramids. A gigantic lion with a human head, it was carved from an outcrop of rock in the time of Pharaoh Chephren, whose pyramid can be seen behind it.*

is something very odd about the pyramid shape itself. A Frenchman named Bovis, visiting the Great Pyramid, found the dead body of a cat lying among the debris in the King's Chamber. Although the air in the chamber was humid, the cat's body had not decayed, but had dried out like a mummy. Bovis later made a scale model of the pyramid in cardboard. He arranged it with the sides facing north, east, west and south – like the Great Pyramid itself – and placed the carcasses of dead animals in it, about a third of the way up inside. For no apparent reason, the bodies did not putrefy but slowly dried out.

A French radiologist named Jean Martial repeated these experiments, with the same results. A fish, for example, lost two-thirds of its weight in thirteen days, but did not rot. In the 1950s an engineer from Prague, Karl Drbal, repeated the experiment with similar results. He also put a used, blunt razor blade inside his model pyramid, and after a week or so it was mysteriously sharp again. The same thing happened with other blades which Drbal tested and he decided that there must be some relation between the shape of the pyramid and the biological, physical and chemical processes occurring within it. He began manufacturing and selling model pyramids as bladesharpeners.

Lyall Watson, the biologist and author of *Supernature*, tried these experiments himself, including the one with the razor blades, and found that they worked. He suggested that the shape of the Great Pyramid might in some way focus or collect energy. Whatever the explanation, people in California started to build pyramidal houses and some enthusiasts went about with small pyramids on their heads, to resharpen their brains. Did the designers of the Great Pyramid, by accident or design, employ a shape which retards the decay of human flesh and assists the process of mummification?

The Great Pyramid

The Great Pyramid is one of the most remarkable constructions ever erected. The tip of it is missing now, but the pyramid originally stood more than 100 feet higher than St Paul's Cathedral in London. Westminster Abbey, St Peter's in Rome and the cathedrals of Florence and Milan could all be fitted together inside the area of its base. It contains well over two million blocks of limestone, weighing on average $2\frac{1}{2}$ tons each and fitted together so closely that, as one archeologist has said, you could hardly slip a card between them. The largest blocks weigh 15 tons and the massive granite roof-slabs of the King's Chamber 50 tons. The whole huge bulk of six million tons stands on an artificially flattened site which deviates from a perfectly level plane by only a little over half an inch (less than 2 cm).

Even more impressive than the size of the Great Pyramid is its geometrical perfection. All the pyramids were designed so that the base was as close as possible to a perfect square, and the sides were aligned as accurately as possible to the cardinal points. The sides of the Great Pyramid are almost exactly the same length. With sides about 9,000 inches (23,000 cm) long at the base, the difference between the longest side and the shortest is less than 8 inches (20 cm). The four corners, consequently, are almost perfect right angles. Not only is the base very nearly a perfect square, but the original height of the pyramid was equal to the radius of a circle whose circumference equalled the perimeter of the base. It looks as if the designers knew the value of *pi* (the ratio between the radius of a circle and its circumference). Furthermore, the four sides of the pyramid face true north, east, south and west with only a tiny deviation from pinpoint accuracy. This could have been achieved only as a result of efficient astronomical observations.

Nobody builds a colossal monument like this without a reason, but no Egyptian documents have survived which explain what the reason was. Egyptian temples were also carefully orientated by the heavenly bodies.

Inscriptions in temples at Denderah and Edfu, for example, show that the line of the walls was marked out after observation of the stars in Ursa Major, but we are not told why. The Egyptians built their astronomical and mathematical knowledge into their pyramids and temples, but did not write it down. It was apparently kept secret among the priests and the ruling class.

Not far from Giza stood Heliopolis, 'the city of the sun' as the Greeks called it. The Egyptians called it On, and it is now a suburb of Cairo. The great temple of the sun at Heliopolis was staffed by a powerful priesthood which interested itself in the study of the heavenly bodies, the measurement of time, and the fixing of an accurate calendar. This priesthood seems to have had a dominating influence on the design of the pyramids.

The priests of Heliopolis were astronomers and mathematicians. The regu-

BELOW *The pyramids at Giza as they are today.*

RIGHT *Copper tools used for stone and woodworking including axes, chisels, saw, awl, adze and bow-drill.*

BELOW *The base being prepared. The ground is levelled down to water in a network of trenches, accurate to 10 cm over 230 m. Men check the alignment of the sides of the pyramid.*

lar movements of the heavenly bodies and the orderly progression of numbers tend to inspire in human beings a sense of an order, a fixed pattern, in the universe. The fact that the whole life of Egypt depended on the regular occurrence of the Nile flood every year probably also contributed to recognition of a universal order governed by forces greater than man. It looks as if the priests expressed their understanding of this order in the pyramids.

Section through the Great Pyramid at Giza shows the passages, various chambers and the Grand Gallery.

ABOVE *The interior of the Grand Gallery. It is thought to have been built to house the giant granite plugs which were used to seal the entrance.*

It was believed in Heliopolis, and widely accepted elsewhere in Egypt, that the earth came into being when a mound emerged from the waters of chaos at the beginning of time. For centuries each Egyptian temple was regarded as a recreation in stone of this primeval mound: 'the island of creation'. It is possible that the pyramid also represented the mound and that it stood for the earth as a whole. This would explain why it was orientated to the cardinal points, for so is the earth itself orientated, and its harmonious geometry would celebrate the perfect proportion of the universal order.

The pyramids were probably also to

ABOVE *Pyramid builders relied on ramps, levers and rollers to move and raise their vast constructions. This twelfth dynasty tomb painting shows over 100 men pulling a 60 ton colossus on its sledge. Note the man pouring liquid under the sledge.*

CENTRE *A team haul a stone up a 10° ramp while men clap and drum a sea-shanty-like rhythm to help them. Others position stones to complete a course; the ramp will then be raised to the level of the next course.*

celebrate the power and stability of Egypt and the glory of the kings, who were the earthly counterparts of the sun-god on high and would go to join him in the sky after death. The shape of the pyramid suggests the idea of rising to the sky, and conversely of the sun-god radiating his power down upon the earth. In effect, each pyramid may have asserted an order on earth in parallel with the order of the universe as a whole. In doing so, it would have the magical purpose of preserving peace and prosperity in Egypt by expressing order and harmony massively in stone.

The relationship between the pharaoh and the great god seems to have been stated in the Sphinx. This gigantic figure of a human-headed lion was carved out of an outcrop of rock in the time of King Chephren. Its face is thought to have been a portrait of Chephren and, later at least, the Sphinx was certainly regarded as an embodiment of the sun-god.

Pyramidiocy

The pyramids have sparked off enough wild theories to fill an asylum, hence the word 'pyramidiocy'. Several writers in the nineteenth century insisted that the designers of the Great Pyramid built into it a detailed prophecy of events extending far into the future from their own time. The prophecy could be recovered by turning various measurements of the pyramid from inches into years. Very few people take this notion seriously any longer, but we are often told that the pyramid's external and internal measurements prove that the Egyptian priests possessed advanced scientific knowledge which was not recovered again until modern times. Among other things, they are supposed to have understood that the earth is round and to have known its precise circumference, its specific density, the mean length of its orbit round the sun, and the speed of light.

All this needs to be taken with large

lumps of salt. It depends on measurements which may be purely coincidental and calculations which may never have entered the heads of the Egyptian priests at all. The same technique has been applied to the cathedrals of Europe, whose dimensions are improbably supposed to enshrine secret scientific knowledge inherited from the ancient world. It is all too easy to 'prove' things by juggling with statistics. St Paul's in London, for instance, stands about 365 feet high and there are 365 days in the year, but there is no need to put this down to anything more than coincidence.

It is also unlikely that the Egyptian priests, with all their scientific knowledge, took a modern scientific attitude to the world and did not believe in the gods. Some writers draw a picture of a cynical priesthood maintaining its privileges by deceiving the Egyptians into accepting fake gods and goddesses. That such a deception could have been kept up successfully for centuries is extremely improbable.

The Tarot and the Mummy's Curse

Another improbable theory traces the origin of the Tarot pack to ancient Egypt. The Tarot is a set of cards resembling modern playing cards, but with twenty-two extra cards, known as 'major trumps'. The extra cards have such titles as the Fool, the Juggler, the Pope, the Lovers, Death, the Hanged Man and the Devil. A Syrian writer of the fourth century AD, Iamblichus, said that initiates into the mysteries of the Egyptian god Osiris were led through a gallery containing twenty-two symbolic pictures of profound spiritual meaning. These pictures, it has been suggested, were the origin of the Tarot's major trumps. However, no trace of Iamblichus's pictures has ever been

found in Egypt, and although the Tarot pack is certainly mysterious and fascinating there is no evidence to link it with Egypt.

Perhaps the best-known 'mystery' of the land of the pharaohs is the story of the curse of Tutankhamen's tomb, which is one of many stories of the same kind. When Cleopatra's Needle – actually an obelisk from the temple at Heliopolis – arrived in London in 1878, there were rumours of a curse which would fall on the heads of those who had removed it from Egypt. With the developing interest in Egyptian archeology, the popular press published lurid tales of curses which would strike down investigators who sacrilegiously disturbed the mummies of the pharaohs. The tales were based on the fact that deadly spells against intruders were indeed inscribed in the tombs.

In 1922 the tomb of Pharaoh Tutankhamen, who died aged eighteen in 1353 BC, was discovered in the Valley of the Kings at Luxor by Lord Carnarvon and Howard Carter. On a tablet in the tomb, or so it is alleged, a curse was written in hieroglyphics: 'Death will slay with his wings whoever disturbs the pharaoh's peace.' Undeterred, Carnarvon and Carter opened the innermost shrine in February 1923, in the presence of about twenty people, to find the mummy of Tutankhamen and an astounding quantity of treasure.

Carnarvon, who was fifty-six, died in Cairo within two months, of pneumonia. For unexplained reasons all the lights in Cairo flickered out at about the moment of his death, and then went on again. By 1929, it is claimed, twenty-

two people who had been involved with Tutankhamen's mummy had died prematurely, thirteen of whom had witnessed the opening of the tomb. Hollywood producers were inspired to create a series of horror films on the theme of 'the Mummy's Curse'.

If the curse really worked, as some people like to think, the obvious question is, why did it not strike down the others who were involved, including Howard Carter, the effective leader of the enterprise, who died at the reasonably ripe age of sixty-five in 1939? The same objection applies to fanciful theories that the Egyptian priests concealed poisons or radioactive materials in the tombs, or somehow harnessed lethal cosmic rays. A more sensible theory looks to bacteria or fungi as possible causes of premature deaths. A Cairo University biologist, Ezzeddin Taha, suggested this in 1962; and soon afterwards died prematurely himself – killed in a car crash – which prompted claims that the priests of ancient Egypt had struck again.

ABOVE *The enigmatic symbols of the Tarot.*

OPPOSITE ABOVE *The tomb of Tutankhamen was the only royal Egyptian tomb to survive almost intact until its discovery in 1922. It contained an astonishing quantity of treasure. Inside a nest of three coffins, the innermost made of solid gold, reposed the mummy of the pharaoh, with a mask of beaten gold.*

OPPOSITE BELOW *Lord Carnarvon and Howard Carter discovered the burying place of Tutankhamen in 1922. They are seen here, talking to a journalist, at the entrance to the tomb. Lord Carnarvon died within two months of the opening of the tomb, allegedly the victim of a curse on anyone who violated the pharaoh's rest.*

25

The Standing Stones

Like the pyramids, the prehistoric tombs, stone circles and standing stones of Europe, seen silent on downland in the sun or looming out of a morning mist, have an eerie quality which has fascinated people for centuries. A powerful atmosphere of magic and the supernatural clings to Carnac and Avebury, to the Rollright Stones in Oxfordshire and Callanish in the Hebrides, and especially to Stonehenge, the most spectacular of them all. Behind this magical reputation, as in Egypt, there seems to lie a distant memory of the remote past, when these mysterious monuments enshrined knowledge and skill which to ordinary people must have seemed awesome and uncanny.

The great megalithic structures (*megalith* from Greek words meaning 'great stone') have stood for four thousand years and more, while millions of human beings have lived and died unregarded. The oldest structures are older than the pyramids and the sheer size and bulk of them is impressive. The largest pillars at Stonehenge not only stand up to 30 feet (9 m) high and weigh up to 50 tons, but they are arranged like doorways and capped with stone lintels, which were heaved up on top of the pillars and held in place with mortise-and-tenon joints. Each of these lintels weighs about the same as seven or eight family saloon cars.

The huge sandstone blocks, the sarsens, were not found obligingly lying about at Stonehenge by the builders. They were dragged there laboriously from 20 miles (30 km) away to the north, on wooden sledges hauled over rollers with ropes by teams of men, and perhaps of oxen. The smaller pillars at Stonehenge, known as bluestones for their colour, were brought from well over 100 miles away, from the Prescelly Mountains in the south-west corner of Wales, apparently from an important religious centre there. They were probably transported as far as possible by boat and then hauled across country.

The interesting question is not so much *how* these feats of engineering were achieved in the total absence of

modern machinery, but *why*. Experiments have shown that the problems of construction can be tackled successfully using only the equipment available to the prehistoric builders – simple picks and shovels, axes and hammers, timbers and ropes. The question is, why did the builders go to so much trouble?

Why, for instance, build the vast complex at Avebury, a few miles west of Stonehenge, covering an area twice the size of the base of the Great Pyramid? Approached along an avenue of standing stones over a mile long, two stone circles stood inside an outer circle of almost 100 hulking monoliths. Outside this again was a ditch 50 feet (15 m) deep and a massive bank of earth, not defensive in purpose because the ditch is *inside* the bank. This formidable earthwork was thrown up using deer-antlers for picks and the shoulder-blades of oxen for shovels.

Just to the south and constructed at about the same date, about 2700 BC, is Silbury Hill, which is not a hill but the biggest man-made mound in Europe. It was skilfully constructed in stepped layers (creating an effect distinctly reminiscent of a flying saucer) and it has been calculated that building it consumed a proportion of the gross national product of the time comparable to that expended by the United States of America on its entire space programme. Tunnelling has revealed no sign that anyone was buried in it and no evidence of what it was for. Or again, at Carnac in Brittany, more than 2,600 standing stones are arranged in parallel lines across miles of country, ten stones or more abreast. Why were they put there with so much toil?

Part of the answer may be that the people who built these things, like the Egyptians, delighted in leaving impress-ive monuments behind them to stand for untold centuries. Beyond this, sites like Stonehenge and Avebury were almost certainly open-air temples. Beyond this again, they were also astronomical observatories of remarkable sophistication.

OPPOSITE ABOVE *The prehistoric stone circles and standing stones have an eerie and magical quality about them and are rich in legend and folklore. Stonehenge, the most famous of them all, was constructed in a succession of phases over many centuries from about 2800 BC.*

OPPOSITE BELOW *Standing stones at Beaghmore, County Tyrone, Ireland. Prehistoric architects placed standing stones in alignments with each other and with points on the horizon, leading the eye to rising or setting positions of the sun or the moon at significant stages in their cycles.*

ABOVE *Men-an-tol, Cornwall. It used to be believed that children who crawled through the hole would be cured of rickets.*

Megalithic Astronomy

It was realized long ago that Stonehenge is orientated to the midsummer sunrise. A man standing at the centre at dawn on Midsummer Day and looking through one of the massive arches to the ceremonial entrance sees the rising sun standing impressively above a 35-ton pillar, known as the Heel Stone. Recently it has become clear that many other features of Stonehenge are related to the movements, or apparent movements, of the sun and the far more complicated movements of the moon.

An imaginary line from the middle of Stonehenge along the axis of the entrance points towards sunrise at the midsummer solstice, on the longest day of the year. A line at right angles to this points to sunrise at the midwinter solstice, on the shortest day of the year. In the reverse direction these lines point

ing for the nineteen-year cycle of the moon, after which the moon's phases start to recur on the same days of the month. Close to the outside edge of Stonehenge is a circle of fifty-six pits, called the Aubrey Holes after the antiquary John Aubrey, who discovered them in the seventeenth century.

Through a complicated system of moving markers from one hole to another, it would have been possible to predict eclipses of the sun and moon, including eclipses not visible from Stonehenge. Standing among the Aubrey Holes were four isolated pillars now known as Station Stones. Lines drawn along the sides of the rectangle formed by Station Stones, or diagonally across it, point to risings of the sun at the solstices and equinoxes (the quarter-days of the year) and to risings of the

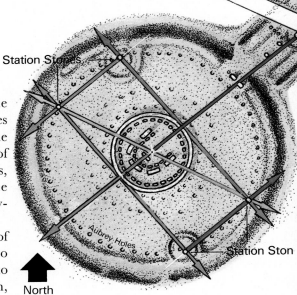

North

ABOVE *Some of the suggested astronomical alignments at Stonehenge.* Red *midsummer sunrise;* Purple *midwinter sunset;* Blue *most northerly and southerly moonrise;* Yellow *other sunrises and sunsets divide the year into further segments.*

BELOW LEFT *Midsummer sunrise seen from the centre of the circle.*

BELOW *Stonehenge today.*

to the midwinter sunset and the midsummer sunset. If Stonehenge had been built a few miles to the north or south, these lines would not cross at right angles. This suggests that Stonehenge was deliberately sited where it is, on the basis of accurate astronomical knowledge. Hence the need to drag the great stones twenty miles to the correct site, rather than build the complex twenty miles further north.

In the third major phase of construction at Stonehenge, about 2000 BC, thirty sarsens were erected in a circle. One of the stones was much smaller than the others and the ring may have represented the twenty-nine and a half days of the lunar month. Inside the circle, nineteen bluestones were later arranged in a horseshoe, possibly stand-

moon at important points in its cycle.

Stonehenge, then, was an astronomical observatory, and possibly a computer for predicting eclipses. Its construction enshrined an advanced knowledge of astronomy, which must have taken many generations of careful observation to achieve. Not only this, but it turns out that a great many other stone circles and standing stones were

positioned in such a way that they can be used for astronomical observations and calculations. The lines of stones at Carnac, for instance, may have formed a kind of giant graph paper for studying events in the sky.

Detailed surveys also indicate that the outlines of the stone circles – some of which are actually elliptical or egg-shaped – were not plotted in any rough

Erecting the stones: the sarsens are pushed down a ramp into a pit, pulled upright and jammed with stones. The lintels are levered on to layers of staging and then slid over on to sarsens.

and ready way, but by precise calculation founded on a substantial knowledge of geometry. They involve a common unit of measurement, the 'megalithic yard' of 2.72 feet (83 cm), and an understanding of properties of triangles previously thought to have been unknown until discovered centuries later by the Greek mathematician Pythagoras.

The Megalithic Architects

The great megalithic complexes were probably built partly out of the sheer fascination of scientific enquiry, and partly out of the need for an accurate calendar to determine the right time for planting seeds and breeding cattle. There is some evidence that the same calendar was in use at this period in places as far apart as Wales and the north of Scotland.

However, the huge size of the stones at some sites suggests that practical

Reconstruction of Stonehenge as it may have looked in about 1300 BC.

considerations were not the only ones involved. There is no need to build a Stonehenge or an Avebury to study the sky and fix the calendar. The sites are separated from the rest of the landscape by their surrounding ditches, which draw a kind of magic circle round them. They have the air of sacred places, and the concern, almost the obsession, of the prehistoric architects with the moon points to a mixture of religion, magic and philosophy as a fundamental motive for their construction. From very early times the cycle of life and death on earth – the birth, growth, decay and death of plants, animals and man – has been linked with the waxings and wanings of the moon in its endless

cycle of births and deaths in the sky.

As in Egypt, the study of astronomy and mathematics is likely to have inspired a sense of an order in the universe, governed by the gods. The megalithic temples seem to have enshrined human understanding of this order, stated in stone, and may well have been intended to have a magical effect in preserving order on earth. The cremated human remains found at Stonehenge, Avebury and other sites imply rituals of some kind, perhaps celebrated at significant stages of the moon's cycle. It does not necessarily follow that human sacrifices were offered in the megalithic temples, but it is a possibility.

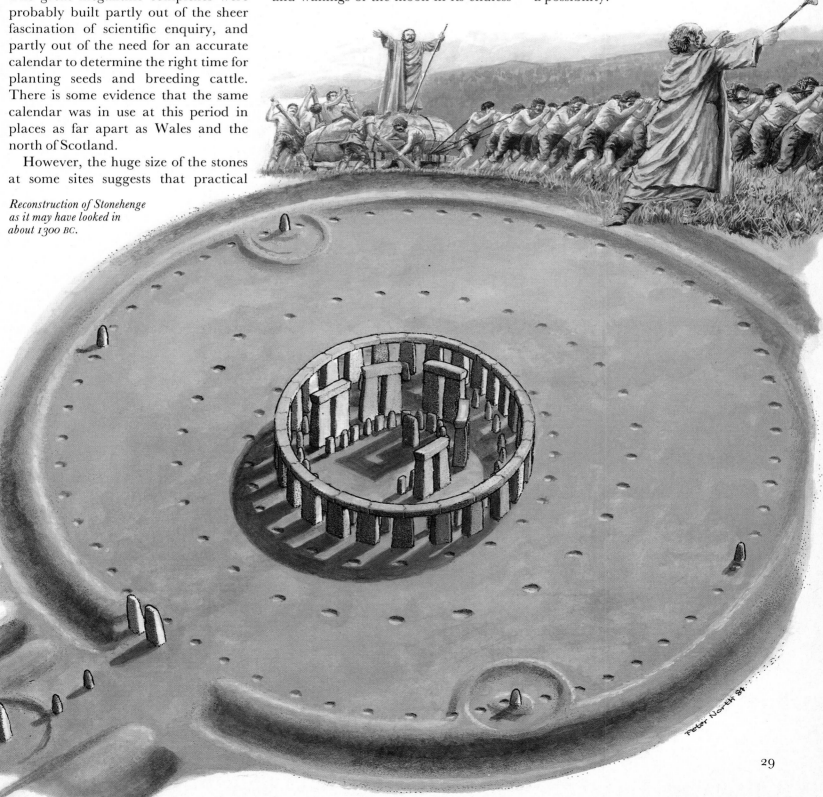

The megalithic astronomers, mathematicians and architects were probably priests, whose prestige depended on their superior understanding of the order established by the gods. They would have handed on their knowledge in secret to their chosen successors, generation by generation. They may have lived in separate communities which were also training colleges – rather like medieval monasteries – near the principal sites, in such places as Woodhenge and Durrington Walls near Stonehenge, and the Sanctuary near Avebury. The priests were part of the ruling class of chieftains and wise men. It was presumably the members of this class who were buried in the great megalithic tombs which are often orientated to the midsummer or midwinter sunrise.

The religion of the time can only be guessed at, but the sun and moon were very likely regarded either as deities or as the vehicles of the powers of the sky. The earth seems to have been a great goddess, the mother of all living things, and there was probably a belief in reincarnation or a life after death of some kind, at least for the ruling class. There would have been a strong concern with the fertility of human beings, animals and crops. One possibility is that, in a stone circle, the circle as a whole is a female symbol and the standing stones which compose it are male symbols. The formal avenue which connects Avebury with the Sanctuary is flanked by a line of stones on one side which appear to be masculine symbols and a line on the other which may be feminine ones.

The Druids

The Druids are popularly linked with Stonehenge and the other megalithic sites and are widely believed to have built them. In reality, the age of megalithic building petered out about 1500 BC, for unknown reasons, while the earliest evidence about the Druids dates from over a thousand years later. All the same, the Druids seem to have inherited something of the scientific knowledge of the megalithic priests centuries before. According to Roman writers, they conducted their rites in groves of trees and forest clearings, but they may have used the old megalithic temples like Stonehenge and Avebury as well.

The Druids were the priests, lawgivers, and wise men of the Celtic tribes in Britain and France in the late centuries BC. They had a grim re-

30

putation in the Roman world because they officiated at the human sacrifices which were a major element of Celtic religion, 'covering their altars with the blood of captives', as the Roman historian Tacitus said, 'and consulting their deities through human entrails.' They also had a reputation for magical power and secret wisdom. They believed in reincarnation and they were interested in astronomy and natural sciences. Some classical writers said they were followers of Pythagoras, which can hardly be correct, but which may mean that they shared with Pythagoras the belief that mathematics held the key to the inner structure of the universe. The Druids kept their knowledge secret. Never written down, it was enshrined in verses which had to be learned by heart. It was said to take twenty years to master and memorize the Druid secrets.

When the Romans conquered France and most of Britain, they put down the Druids. In doing so, they seem to have suppressed, along with human sacrifice, an old tradition of scientific knowledge and an old understanding of the world.

Lines of Power

According to the archeologists, after the massive stones of megalithic temples had been hauled to the site, each was laboriously raised on end with levers and ramps until its base rested in the pit dug to receive it. However, there is an entirely different and startling explanation of how the stones were erected. The megalithic engineers, so this theory runs, had psychic control of powerful currents of electro-magnetic energy in the earth. They simply spoke a word of command and the great stones flew obediently through the air to the chosen site and settled themselves down there!

An old legend, going back to the twelfth century or earlier, says that Stonehenge was magically transported through the air to Salisbury Plain from Ireland by Merlin, the great enchanter. The modern theory, however, has its roots in the discoveries of a kind of modern Merlin – an elderly photographer and naturalist named Alfred Watkins. Sitting in his car one day in 1921 and looking idly at a map, he saw a vision of a network of straight lines running across the countryside and linking together prehistoric sites, churches and other landmarks. Following up the idea on maps and on the ground, he found that many features of the landscape seemed to be arranged in straight lines. They included prehistoric burial mounds, stone circles and standing stones, old settlements, churches, holy wells, wayside crosses and old marker stones, pools, fords, and notches, clumps of trees and beacon sites on hills.

Watkins called his lines *leys* (pronounced 'lays'). He thought they were prehistoric tracks, laid down at a time when people found their way across country by going straight from one landmark to another. He also suggested that some of them were aligned to the sun or the stars. Watkins died in 1935, but enthusiasts have since found thousands more leys. Obviously, any two points on a map can be connected by a straight line. To qualify as a ley, the line should touch at least four significant points in a distance of ten miles or so.

The theory to explain leys has changed, because it is most unlikely that prehistoric man marched straight from one landmark to the next. He would take the easiest routes, and very old tracks which have survived, like the Ridgeway in southern England, do not run straight. The leys are now claimed to be lines of force, created as the earth cooled in the almost immeasurably distant past. Additionally, they are lines of 'psychic energy'. Places like Stonehenge or the castle mound at Cambridge or Cley Hill, near Warminster in Wiltshire, where several lines converge, are ley-centres, rather like power stations, concentrating huge quantities of energy. The people of prehistoric times, who lived closer to nature than modern man, and had far more highly developed psychic faculties, were aware of this web of energy, which they marked out on the ground and harnessed. According to some writers, they gained their knowledge of these power-currents from Atlantis or, according to others, from missionaries from outer space.

ABOVE LEFT *At Callanish on the island of Lewis a tall stone pillar stands at the centre of a circle of thirteen stones. Lines of stones run out from the circle to the north, east, south and west, making a cross shape. The alignments are related to the cycle of the moon.*

Leys, Triangles and Zodiacs

Megalithic builders often placed standing stones outside a circle to lead the eye to a point on the horizon – a hill or notch or mound – where the sun or the moon rose or set at some significant point of its cycle. The theory of leys goes far beyond this, and the main problem with leys is that it might be nothing more than a coincidence when features of the landscape fall in straight lines. Far too many leys carry little conviction, but there are some impressive alignments in Cornwall, near Land's End, in an area rich in prehistoric monuments. From the stone circle of Boscawen-un, for example, five standing stones, three still erect and two fallen, were found to run in a straight line for about three miles. Each marker is visible from the next, but the line seems to have no practical astronomical purpose. Similarly, another straight line with no apparent astronomical reference can be drawn from the centre of Stonehenge to the prehistoric earthwork of Old Sarum and on through Salisbury Cathedral to the edge of

prehistoric Clearbury Ring. The total distance is about twelve miles.

Other leys, or alleged leys, are astronomically orientated. If the midsummer sunrise axis of Stonehenge is extended to the north-east, it skirts the edge of the earthwork at Sidbury Hill and continues to the hilltop of Inkpen Beacon and the Winterbourne earthwork. Extended the other way, to the south-west, the line runs to the prehistoric settlement of Grovely Castle and crosses the Cerne Abbas Giant, a famous hill-figure of unknown date in Dorset, to finish at Puncknowle Beacon on the coast.

Some leys form equilateral or isosceles triangles. Stonehenge, Old Sarum, and Grovely Castle lie in an equilateral triangle whose sides are six miles long. The so-called Great Isosceles Triangle of England has its apex at Arbor Low, a stone circle and redoubtable ley-centre in Derbyshire, and its other corners about 150 miles away at Othery church, near Glastonbury, and West Mersea on the Essex coast. The celebrated White Horse of Uffington, a superb prehistoric hill-carving, is said to form an isosceles triangle with the white horses on hillsides at Pewsey and Cherhill in Wiltshire.

The Pewsey and Cherhill white horses were made far more recently than the Uffington one, which illustrates another difficulty about leys. The points they connect together may be hundreds or even thousands of years apart in date. It is true that in the early days of Christianity, churches were often built on pagan, pre-Christian sacred sites, so as to Christianize them; but is it really likely that Salisbury Cathedral, built in the thirteenth century, was deliberately planted on the prehistoric Stonehenge-Old Sarum-Clearbury Ring line? There is no evidence that anybody in medieval times was aware of such alignments.

In some places giant zodiacs have been laid out in the landscape, or so it is claimed. Viewed from the air, the patterns formed by hills, streams, hedges, banks and ditches, tracks and roads, represent the animals and other symbolic figures of complete zodiac circles. The best-known one is the Glastonbury Zodiac, which is ten miles across. Other zodiacs have been discovered at Kingston in Surrey, Nuthampstead in Hertfordshire, Holderness in Yorkshire, and at Ffarmers and Pumpsaint, near Lampeter in Wales.

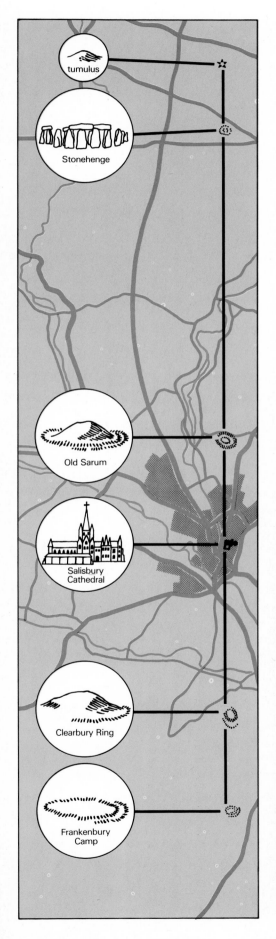

Looked at with even a mildly doubting eye, the zodiacs fail to impress. It is too easy to imagine shapes in contour lines and other features of maps and aerial photographs. The triangles also seem more coincidental than meaningful.

As with pyramidiocy, leys have been brought into disrepute by far-fetched theories and inaccurate claims. Even so, there may be something in them. First set aside the wilder notions – zodiacs, the invisible power-grid, and the picture of the huge stones lumbering through the air like prehistoric jumbo jets. Then confine the evidence to prehistoric landmarks and an interesting possibility emerges. It is that megalithic builders sometimes aligned circles, standing stones and other constructions with natural features in straight lines, at least over comparatively short distances. If they did, it was presumably in connection with their mathematical and scientific interests, and perhaps as an expression of their concept of universal order. However, until the alignments are checked by someone whose reputation as a surveyor carries adequate weight, the case for leys will remain in doubt.

OPPOSITE *At Carnac in Brittany hundreds upon hundreds of stones stretch away to the horizon.*

LEFT *The Clearbury Ring/Stonehenge ley can be extended in both directions to ancient earthworks, giving a line running north-north-west/ south-south-east for 18½ miles.*

BELOW *The White Horse of Uffington is said to form an isosceles triangle with two other white horses of much more recent date, at Pewsey and Cherhill.*

The Nazca Lines

There is no doubt at all about the existence of a huge complex of lines and patterns on the ground in the desert near Nazca in Peru. The lines were made by removing the stones which carpet the ground, to expose the yellowish-white soil beneath. There are thousands of straight lines, some more than five miles long. They are laid out with remarkable accuracy, scarcely deviating from true even when a line crosses a hill or a gully. Straightness was evidently important to whoever designed them. Some of the lines are parallel, some converge, some radiate out from centres in small piles of boulders. There are also spirals, triangles and quadrilaterals, and hundreds of enormous figures of birds, fish, spiders, snakes, whales, monkeys and other animals.

This complex, which has been called the world's largest work of art, was made before the Incas ruled Peru, but long after the megalithic age in Europe. It is believed to date from some time between 400 BC and AD 900, and to have taken several centuries to complete.

A strange thing about the lines is that they cannot be seen properly from anywhere on the ground. They are viewed to the best advantage from about 600 feet up in the air. This has inspired suggestions that they were meant to be seen by visiting astronauts in flying saucers. There is a possibility that the Nazcans who constructed the lines viewed them from smoke balloons. The principle of hot air ballooning has apparently long been known in South America, and in 1975 two observers flew over the site in a smoke balloon constructed entirely from materials available to the ancient Nazcans.

Why the Nazcans wanted to build the complex and hover over it in balloons (if they did) remains a mystery. Did it somehow express their understanding of the universe, an understanding into which those who viewed it were initiated? Was it laid out in honour of gods in the sky, who would look down and see it and be pleased? Some of the straight lines are aligned to sunrises and sunsets at the solstices and equinoxes, and

others with the stars; and some of the animal figures are thought to be connected with the calendar and the seasons. This suggests that, in part at least, the complex was a combination of astronomical observatory, calendar, and magical machine for preserving order and prosperity on earth. Most of the lines, however, seem to have no reference to the sky or the calendar. There is no fully convincing explanation of the Nazca lines as yet, but they do bear witness to a determination to mark out patterns on the earth's surface – an impulse shared by the megalithic builders in Europe.

OPPOSITE *In the desert between the Ica and Nazca valleys in Peru a giant's picture-book of animals and birds, straight lines and geometrical figures was drawn on the ground many centuries ago. The figures can only be seen properly from about 600 feet up in the air. This drawing represents a spider.*

ABOVE *Drawing of a monkey. The lines were made by removing the stones which carpet the ground, to lay bare the whitish soil beneath. There are thousands of lines, some of them running straight with astonishing accuracy for miles.*

RIGHT *This figure of a hummingbird is 100 yards (90 m) long. It is possible that the people who made the desert lines viewed them from balloons, but why they wanted to make them in the first place remains a puzzling mystery.*

The Secret of the Maze

On a far smaller scale, the same impulse can be seen in mazes, where complicated patterns are cut in turf or marked out with hedges or stones. Hedge mazes, like the famous one at Hampton Court in London, first became fashionable in the sixteenth century and were intended only for amusement. However, a few examples of the older type of turf maze can still be seen in Britain though many others have been destroyed. These mazes were often called Troys, Troy Towns or Walls of Troy. The explanation is supposed to lie in an old tale that the walls of Troy were built in such a way that attackers became trapped in their labyrinthine intricacies, but this has the air of being a tradition invented to account for something whose true origin and purpose had been forgotten.

In the old days mazes were used for dances, processions and games, all with an element of ritual in them. In some medieval churches a maze was laid out in tiles on the floor. There is a famous one in Chartres Cathedral, which is 40 feet (12 m) across. It is said, though on doubtful authority, that worshippers would tread a maze in a church as a symbolic pilgrimage, the heart of the maze being called Jerusalem or Heaven, and some would follow the winding pattern painfully on their knees as a way of punishing themselves for their sins.

There are two major varieties of maze. The 'puzzle' type contains confusing side-tracks and blind alleys, and the path to the centre and out again is hard to find. The other type consists of a single path which twists and bends back on itself until at last it reaches the centre. Following this kind of maze, you cover the maximum ground without treading in the same place twice. There is no way of getting lost in it and it is difficult to see how it could ever have

been intended purely for amusement.

Both types of maze suggest an analogy with human life: a course over a devious route to a hidden goal. But what is it that lies at the centre? Death? Immortality? Ultimate truth? An encounter with something appallingly dangerous, typified by the Minotaur, the monster which in legend lurked in the Cretan labyrinth? One thing which is certainly at the heart of the maze, when you have trodden the winding path to it, is *you*. Perhaps what you find there is yourself, and the monster is your animal nature which has to be slain, as Theseus in legend killed the Minotaur.

The fascination which mazes still hold for us – their air of deep significance and even danger – may be a legacy of the time when the pattern of the maze was sacred and uncanny, because it held the key to the secret of life. Many mazes consist of spirals, and the spiral is symbolically associated with the recurring pattern of life – ebb and flow, waxing and waning, sunrise and sunset, growth and death and new life. It is interesting that spirals are often found carved on megaliths, and the art of the Celts, who succeeded the megalithic peoples in western Europe, made much use of spiral patterns. Mazes may once have been sacred centres where rituals were performed, connected with the mysteries of life and death. It may be that to follow the winding path to the centre of the maze and return again was symbolically and magically to conquer death, to die and be reborn again.

OPPOSITE *A maze cut in turf at Troy Farm, near Somerton, Oxfordshire. Old mazes are often called Troys or connected with places named Troy. In the old days they were used for dances, processions and games, all with an element of ritual in them.*

RIGHT *Maze pattern at Lucca Cathedral, Italy, and (above) a rare photograph of the maze on the floor of Chartres Cathedral. It is said that worshippers used to follow the winding pattern painfully on their knees as a penance for their sins.*

Glastonbury and the Grail

Some people believe that an ancient man-made spiral path winds seven times round Glastonbury Tor and that pilgrims once trod the path to the summit. The Glastonbury maze is not much more convincing than the Glastonbury Zodiac, but both are products of the magnetic attraction that Glastonbury holds for many people, an attraction so strong as to raise the question whether some places are charged with a peculiar force. Glastonbury's magnetism is linked with its legendary antiquity as a Christian centre and its connections with King Arthur and the Grail.

Glastonbury Tor is a conical hill which rises steeply from low-lying ground. Until the surrounding marshes were drained in the Middle Ages, it stood on what was virtually an island among tangled swamps, and its uncanny impressiveness – still evident today – may have made Glastonbury a pagan sacred site long before it was a Christian one. On top of the Tor stands the ruined church of St Michael, in Christian tradition the leader of the angels of God against the powers of darkness. Below lie the ruins of Glastonbury Abbey. The abbey was closed down by Henry VIII in 1539 and the last abbot was hanged on the summit of the Tor.

Centuries before this, Glastonbury had acquired a reputation as the site of the oldest Christian foundation in Britain. In the abbey grounds stood a humble building of wattle and daub – the Old Church, dedicated to the Virgin Mary, burned down in a disastrous fire in 1184. It was believed to be the first church ever built in the British Isles.

Glastonbury Tor, crowned by the tower of the ruined chapel of St Michael. According to one theory, the terraces which spiral round the hill are a man-made, maze-like processional path to the summit (though in fact numerous other hills in Somerset have similar terraces).

The story was that Christianity first came to Britain in AD 63, when twelve missionaries led by Joseph of Arimathea arrived at Glastonbury. They settled among the swamps, and there they built the Old Church. The name Joseph of Arimathea is significant, for he is mentioned briefly in the New Testament as a rich Jew who arranged for Jesus' burial after the Saviour's death on the cross. In medieval legend, however, he was the first Keeper of the Holy Grail.

The legends of the Grail have an enthralling atmosphere of mystery, of some tremendous secret which stays tantalizingly in the shadows just beyond the mind's grasp. The Grail was a talisman of impressive sanctity and power, the cup of the Last Supper from which Jesus gave his disciples the wine at the first Mass. The wine was his blood, shed on the cross to save men from death; the Grail was the vessel of union with God and immortality in heaven, and it held the key to the ultimate meaning of life. According to legend it was preserved and guarded in secret, and the knights of King Arthur's court rode out in search of it.

King Arthur is the most famous of all legendary British heroes and Glastonbury is not far from Cadbury Castle, an old hill fort which may have been the original Camelot, Arthur's headquarters. In 1191 the monks of Glastonbury claimed to have discovered Arthur's body, buried in the abbey cemetery. Once Arthur and Joseph of Arimathea had both been linked with Glastonbury, it is not surprising that the Grail was too. A story grew up that Joseph of Arimathea brought the Grail with him to Glastonbury and, to keep the sacred cup safe from profane hands, he buried it somewhere at the foot of the Tor. Nowadays the Grail is often said to lie deep in the spring known as Chalice Well, whose water has a reddish hue, as if tinged with the holy blood.

According to a variant of the legend, Joseph and his companions did not build the Old Church, but found it already standing when they came to Glastonbury. It had been built with his own hands by Jesus himself, who spent part of his boyhood at the village of Priddy in the Mendip Hills, not far from Glastonbury!

It would be splendid if these stories

were true, but they are sadly unsupported by evidence. There is nothing impossible in the idea of Glastonbury as a sacred site from a very early date, but it is improbable that Jesus was in Somerset in his youth, doubtful whether the body the monks found was Arthur's, and unlikely that the cup of the Last Supper came to Glastonbury, or ever survived at all. On the other hand, there is no denying the attraction of the place and the sacredness which seems to invest it. Perhaps it is all a delusion. Perhaps those who know the legends clothe Glastonbury in a romantic aura of their own making. Or is it perhaps that, in some way not yet understood, when a place is held sacred the emotions focused on it over the years impress themselves upon it and create a spellbinding atmosphere that is intangible, yet real? If so, this would help to account for the magnetic attraction of Stonehenge, Avebury, Carnac, and many other ancient sacred places.

The Miracles at Lourdes

Another place which has a powerful sacred atmosphere, of much more recent origin, is the great Roman Catholic pilgrimage centre of Lourdes in the French Pyrenees, which draws two million visitors every year. Lourdes is famous for the miraculous healings which have occurred there since the Virgin Mary was seen in a succession of visions by a girl of fourteen, Marie-Bernarde Soubirous, who was canonized as St Bernadette. In 1858, in a shallow cave known as the Grotto, Bernadette saw a woman in a white dress with a blue sash, and with yellow roses on her bare feet. The figure vanished, but Bernadette saw it seventeen times more. In the later stages crowds of interested spectators accompanied her to the Grotto and watched her talking to someone invisible. Bernadette called the figure 'Acquero', meaning 'that' or 'that one', and later 'the Lady'.

On one occasion, the Lady told

Bernadette to drink at the spring. There was no spring at Lourdes, but the spectators saw Bernadette scratching at the floor of the cave, and water seeping into the hole she made – she had discovered a spring. People soon began to collect the water in bottles and before long came the first reports of miraculous cures.

In 1866, after a careful investigation, the Roman Catholic authorities declared that Bernadette had truly seen Mary, the Mother of God. Bernadette finally fled from the glare of publicity to a convent far away from Lourdes and died there in 1879, aged thirty-five. No one doubted her honesty at the time, and there is no reason to doubt it now, though whether she really saw the Virgin Mary or whether she experienced a series of hallucinations is open to question.

The number of sufferers who have been healed at Lourdes is greatly exceeded by the number who have not. One explanation of the cures, obviously, is to attribute them to God. An alternative possibility is that the faith of some patients is so strong, reinforced by the hallowed atmosphere of the shrine, that in effect they cure themselves. However, some odd cases have been reported, like that of a paralysed atheist who challenged God to cure the blind boy next to him, and then discovered that he was healed but the boy was not.

Quite apart from physical healing, there is ample evidence that people who go to Lourdes come away feeling better psychologically for the experience. Numerous visitors, including some who were initially sceptical, have said that the place has an indefinable quality of well-being about it.

ABOVE LEFT Vision of the Holy Grail, *detail of a tapestry by William Morris to a design by Sir Edward Burne-Jones. Legend has it that the Grail, the cup of the Last Supper, was brought to Glastonbury in the first century AD and buried deep in the spring now known as Chalice Well.*

LEFT *Marie-Bernarde Soubirous, canonized as St Bernadette, was born at Lourdes in 1844 and was regarded as a backward child. It was her visions of the Virgin Mary which transformed Lourdes from a backwater into a great pilgrimage centre. She died at the age of thirty-five in 1879.*

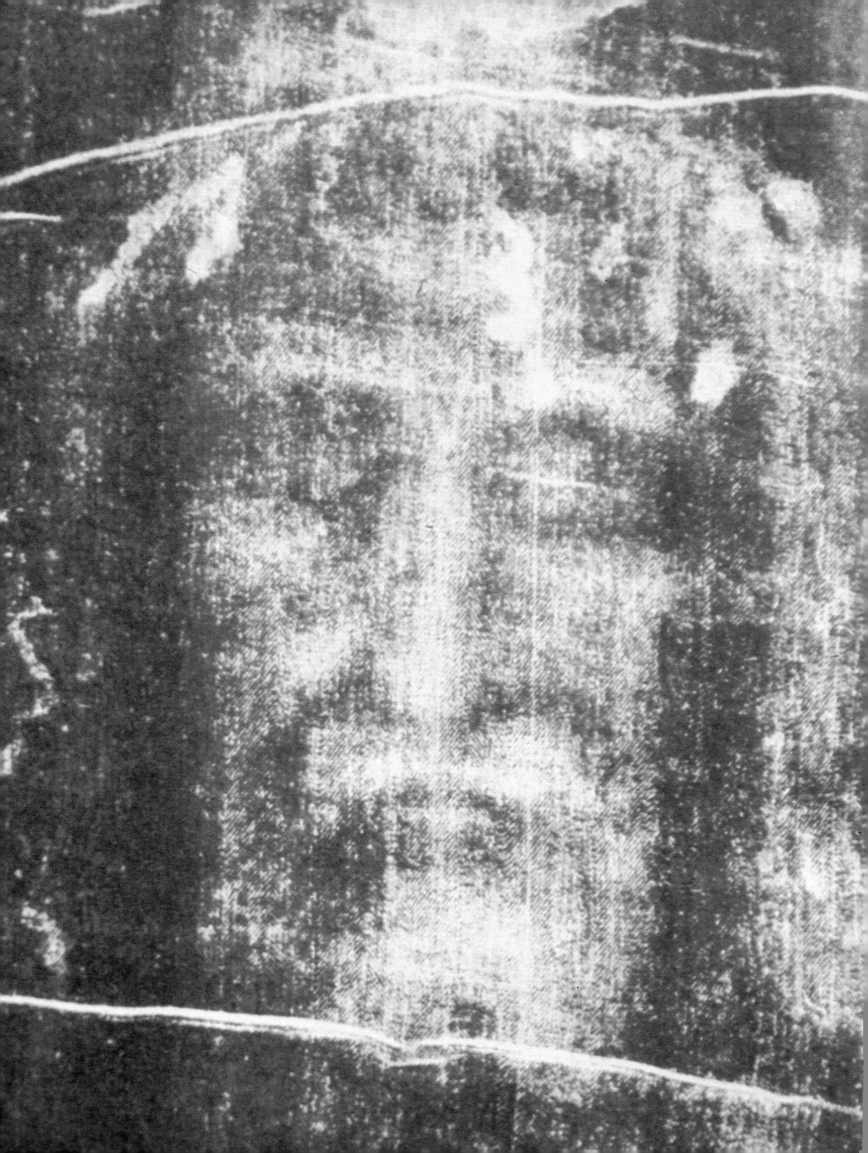

The Holy Shroud of Turin

Like some places, some objects seem to possess a curious power. In the Middle Ages, objects closely associated with Christ, the Virgin Mary or the saints – and especially the dead bodies of saints, or parts of them – were regarded as sacred relics, imbued with supernatural power. Many stories are told of people being healed by contact with relics or by visiting the tomb of a saint, and again it seems possible that the intensity of belief and emotion concentrated upon an object of this kind might surround it with an ambience which is sensed by observers. However, relics raise another interesting possibility, that an object may acquire something of the personal force of its owner and retain it after the owner's death. In this case, a relic of a person of unusual holiness might radiate an inspiring spiritual energy. This has certainly been widely believed, not only in Christianity but in many other religions.

A particularly fascinating relic is the Holy Shroud, believed to be Christ's winding sheet, which is kept in Turin Cathedral in Italy. It appears, astonishingly, to be a kind of photograph of Jesus. The Shroud has been the object of much attention since 1898, when it was first photographed. Since 1973 it has been subjected to various scientific tests.

The Shroud is a piece of linen cloth, 14 feet 3 inches long and 3 feet 7 inches wide (434 × 109 cm). Ivory-coloured with age, it bears faint brownish marks. These marks show up more clearly in photographic negatives, when they are seen to be the imprint of the body of a man who had been crucified. He was wrapped in the cloth in such a way that imprints of both the front and the back of the body are visible. The body bears the wounds of nails through the wrists and of a nail driven through both feet. There are also the marks of a severe flogging and lacerations round the head made by sharp points, consistent with a cap of thorns having been pressed down on the head. There are bruises on the shoulders, consistent with the marks of carrying a heavy cross, and lacerations of the knees consistent with heavy falls.

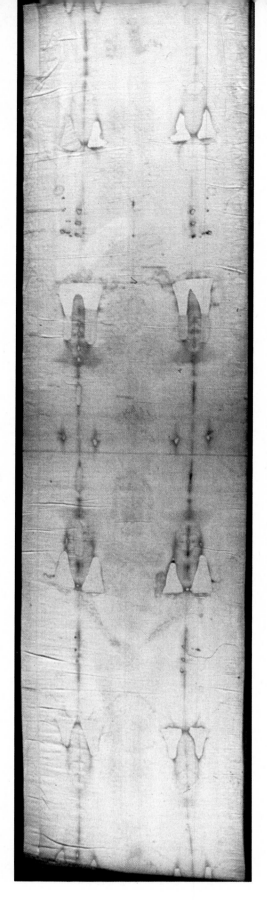

ABOVE *The Holy Shroud, believed to be Christ's winding sheet.*

OPPOSITE *The face on the Shroud. Is this a photograph of Jesus?*

Finally, there is a wound in the right side between the fifth and sixth ribs, which fits the New Testament account of a soldier piercing Christ's body on the cross with a spear.

The man of the Shroud stood just over 6 feet tall (181 cm). He was powerfully built and well proportioned, with a beard and long hair. Medical experts put his age at between thirty and forty-five. He is naked and his eyes are closed in death.

Is what we see in the Shroud the face of the dead Jesus? All the marks of wounds are consistent with the details in the New Testament. The scientific tests are not conclusive, but nor do they rule out the possibility. The known history of the Shroud goes back to the fourteenth century, when it was in France, but its history before that is anybody's guess. Radiocarbon dating has not been attempted because it would entail destroying a piece of the fabric, and in any case it would only provide an extremely rough date. Analysis of dust samples indicates that the Shroud was in Palestine at some stage in its career. Apparently, coins were placed on the dead man's eyes, and in 1980 Professor Filas of Loyola University, Chicago, announced that tiny marks on the cloth had been almost certainly identified as impressions of a Roman coin minted between AD 30 and 32, when Pontius Pilate was governor of Palestine.

The case for the Shroud is clearly impressive. One puzzle is the question of how the marks became imprinted on the cloth, which seems to be a kind of photographic negative. Other shrouds of great age bear similar marks, though without the Shroud's clarity and detail. It has been suggested that the image on the Shroud was created by an intense radiation from inside – from the body. According to the New Testament, when the disciples came to Jesus's tomb the grave clothes were lying empty and the body had disappeared. Is the truth behind the Christian story of the Resurrection that a burst of mysterious power dissolved the body and imprinted its image on the Shroud? Whether continuing tests will provide an answer remains to be seen, but we shall probably never know the whole truth about the Holy Shroud.

Time and Space

Time and Space

The idea of places and objects radiating a mysterious force that affects human beings may or may not be true, but it is at least less outrageous than it was a hundred years ago. According to modern physics the world is a much odder place than we realize, and the famous British biologist J.B.S. Haldane once remarked, 'the universe is not only stranger than we imagine; it is stranger than we *can* imagine.'

It does not follow that any theory, however extravagant, deserves to be taken seriously, but the nineteenth-century 'laws of nature' have been almost entirely discarded. With them has gone most of our ordinary conventional understanding of the world. When a physicist sits down to eat his breakfast at a table, he treats the table as a solid object on which, if he likes, he can rest his elbows. In his capacity as a physicist, however, he does not regard the table as a solid object at all. It consists almost entirely of empty space in which minute particles or waves of energy whirl about, separated from each other by distances which, in relation to them, are vast.

The old belief was that things existed in a solid, four-square way in the three dimensions of space and the separate dimension of time. Now they exist in the interconvertible concepts of mass and energy in the continuum of space-time. Whether space-time is infinite or whether it has boundaries, a beginning and an end, is uncertain. Either way it is puzzling, but theoretical physics has moved on far beyond this point to such mind-boggling concepts as negative mass, negative energy and parallel universes.

According to one well-known theory, there are 'black holes' in space, formed by stars which have contracted, becoming ever smaller and denser until no light or radiation can escape from them. They have consequently become unobservable, but they still exert a gravitational pull on other bodies. A spaceship sucked into a black hole would disappear. Would it collapse to a point of 'infinite density' (whatever that may

be) or would it appear as a 'white hole' in another universe? The question is an example of the sheer weirdness of modern physics.

PREVIOUS PAGES *Horsehead nebula, NGC 2024 in Orion.*

ABOVE *A few days after the surrender of the Confederate armies, President Lincoln was shot through the head in his box at the theatre on the night of 14 April 1865, and died the following morning. The assassin was an actor named John Wilkes Booth, a fanatic for the Southern cause.*

OPPOSITE BELOW *The presidential election of 1880 was won by the Republican candidate, Senator James A. Garfield. He was inaugurated in March 1881, but in July was shot in a Washington railway station and died the following September.*

OPPOSITE ABOVE *Governor William McKinley of Ohio won the presidential election of 1896 for the Republicans and was re-elected in 1900. In September the following year he went to Buffalo to deliver a speech, was shot by an anarchist fanatic named Leon Czolgosz and died of his wounds a week later.*

Time and Coincidence

Another strange concept is the notion of time running backwards. According to one theory, certain particles called positrons are electrons which, astonishingly, are moving backwards in time while the other electrons are moving forwards. Equally astonishingly, if time may not always flow in the same direction, it apparently does not always run at the same speed. There is experimental evidence to confirm Einstein's theory that a clock runs slower when it is moving past an observer than when it is stationary relative to the observer. The effects are only appreciable at extremely high speeds, but the consequence is that if an astronaut is fired off into space at great speed, spends some years travelling in space and then returns home at

46

great speed, he will have aged less than the people on the ground. To the astronaut time has seemed to run normally but, relative to him, clocks on the ground have run faster. Hence the science-fiction stories of astronauts returning from a long journey in space to find their contemporaries on earth white with age or long dead, while they themselves are still young.

Paradoxes like this make nonsense of our conventional view of time, which is also called in question by the results of ESP (extra-sensory perception) experiments. Some people have a remarkable ability to forecast future events – a run

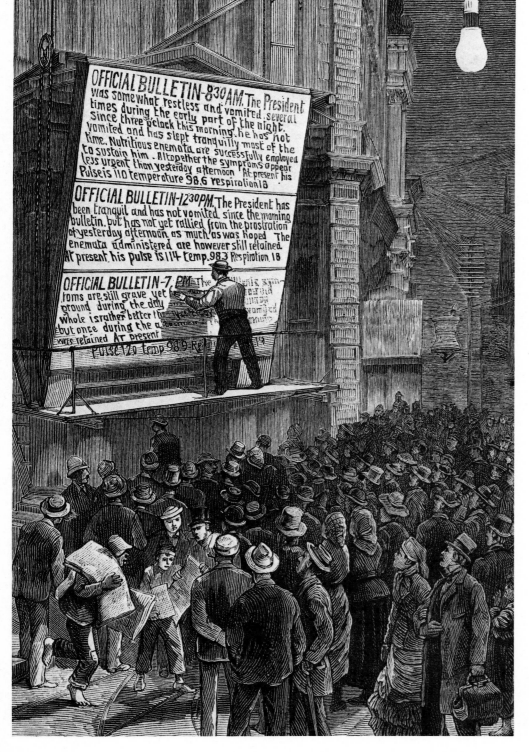

of cards, for instance, or the fall of dice, or the order in which lamps will light up – and get the right answers far more often than could be expected to occur by chance. There are also numerous cases of successful 'hunches', where someone becomes convinced in a way which goes beyond logic that a particular event will soon occur, and it does. Again, it is obvious that some people are luckier than others. They win at gambling much more often, or they have a knack of being in the right place at the right time, or things consistently go right for them, for no apparent reason. Does what we call 'luck' or 'hunch' really conceal an ability to sense the direction in which events are moving? If so, where does this leave our conventional belief that the future is largely unpredictable, because it depends on extremely complex chains of cause and effect? And where does it leave our conventional assumption that our own decisions help to determine future events?

This leads to the puzzling subject of coincidences, events which seem to be connected, but not by cause and effect. An example is the curious fact that since 1840 every President of the United States elected at twenty-year intervals has died in office. The list is: William Henry Harrison, elected 1840, died 1841; Abraham Lincoln, elected 1860, assassinated 1865; James A. Garfield, elected 1880, assassinated 1881; William McKinley, elected 1900, assassinated 1901; Warren G. Harding, elected 1920, died 1923; Franklin D. Roosevelt, elected 1940, died 1945; John F. Kennedy, elected 1960, assassinated 1963. The next election in this ominous series fell in 1980, when Ronald Reagan was elected . . .

It scarcely seems likely that seven American Presidents died in office *because* they won the elections of these particular years. A chain of events like this raises the question of whether, contrary to the nineteenth-century picture of the universe, events are not related to each other only by cause and effect. Perhaps there is some other natural law at work, which we do not understand and possibly do not even observe in operation much of the time, because it is outside our accustomed frame of reference. The Austrian biologist Paul Kammerer, who compiled an extensive collection of coincidences over twenty years, thought that the coincidences we notice are only the tip of an iceberg and that they indicate the presence of a principle operating independently of physical causation. The psychiatrist C. G. Jung, the great Austrian physicist Wolfgang Pauli, and the distinguished writer Arthur Koestler have also suggested that coincidences are the product of some non-causal, non-physical factor in nature.

ABOVE *Senator John F. Kennedy was elected the thirty-fifth President of the United States in 1960, and the curious and fatal chain of coincidences still held. Greatly admired and loved, he was shot while driving through Dallas, Texas, in a motorcade on 22 November 1963.*

ABOVE RIGHT *The first major battle of the Civil War in Britain was fought at Edgehill in Warwickshire in 1642, both sides claiming the victory after a bloody encounter. Soon afterwards rumours spread that local people had seen the battle being fought again by phantom armies.*

Spectral Armies

Peculiarities of time and space, not yet understood, are among the possible explanations of mysterious experiences which have been reported so often that it is difficult to dismiss them all out of hand. A few years ago, for example, a man at work in a cellar in York was staggered to see a patrol of Roman legionaries, one of them on horseback, emerge through one wall of the cellar, march across it and disappear through the opposite wall. They took no notice whatever of him, but one thing which stayed in his memory was that he could

not see the feet of the marching legionaries. It turned out on investigation that an old Roman road ran beneath the building, and its surface was a little way below the cellar floor.

In 1961 a young couple were sitting in a car on the Roman road known as the Icknield Way. They heard the tramp of marching men but then, when the soldiers came by, were astonished to see that they were Roman legionaries. The same thing is said to have happened to a group of people on the same road a few months later.

Something extraordinary happened a few years earlier to a lady living in Angus, Scotland, close to the site of the

battle of Nechtansmere. This battle was fought in AD 685 between the Northumbrians and the Picts; the Northumbrians were decisively defeated and their king was killed. Late one night in 1950 the lady was walking home with her dog when she saw flaming torches some distance ahead of her. As she walked on, she saw figures carrying torches closer to her and the dog began to growl. Judging from her description of their costume and behaviour, what she saw was the aftermath of the battle, with the Picts searching among the corpses on the battlefield for their dead. The figure nearest to her would bend down and turn a body over to see its face, then leave it and go on to the next one. The figures took no notice of her, and at the time she was more concerned that her dog might start barking and wake the village than that she was seeing something that had happened more than a thousand years before.

How is it possible for episodes from the past to be seen in this way? No one knows, but reports of experiences of this kind go back for centuries. In 1642, during the Civil War, a ferociously bloody battle was fought at Edgehill in Warwickshire between the Cavalier and Roundhead armies. Soon afterwards some of the local people said they had seen the battle being fought again.

They had heard the clash of steel, the roar of the drums, the thunder of cannon and the moans of the wounded and dying, and seen the rival banners carried into the fray. King Charles I sent a committee of gentlemen to investigate. They reported that the story was true and that they themselves had seen the two armies fighting and recognized among the combatants many of those who had been killed at Edgehill, including the Royalist standard-bearer, Sir Edmund Verney.

Ghosts at Versailles

A fascinating case of more recent vintage occurred early in this century. In 1901 two English ladies, Miss C.A.E. Moberly and Miss E.M. Jourdain, visited the Petit Trianon at Versailles where the ill-fated Marie Antoinette, Queen of France, played at being a dairymaid before the French Revolution. Without realizing it at the time, they saw various features of the grounds and gardens which were not in fact there in 1901, but *had* been there a century and more before, in 1770. They also saw figures in eighteenth-century costume, including two men in greenish clothes and three-cornered hats, and a man in a heavy black cloak, his dark face marked by smallpox. The two ladies were so reluctant to talk about the experience that it was a week before they discussed it with each other. Miss Jourdain later recalled 'the heavy dreaminess' of the atmosphere and 'a feeling of depression and loneliness about the place.'

Several other visitors to Versailles have had similar experiences. In 1938 a lady who was walking in the park of the Petit Trianon on a fine sunny day saw a man and a woman in peasant costume of the late eighteenth century pulling a small cart loaded with logs. The cart made no noise and the figures passed her in complete silence. Surprised, she turned round to watch them and, she said, they gradually vanished. In 1949 an English family from Westmoreland visited Versailles, and in the grounds they saw a woman in a crinoline and a large picture hat, with her dark hair falling in ringlets to her shoulders. There was nothing ghostly about her, though they thought her costume eccentric, but she too disappeared.

Hauntings, Time and Reincarnation

Versailles, it seems, is haunted – or, to put it another way, it is a place where visitors sometimes see figures, landscapes and episodes from the past. Innumerable other places, ranging from stately homes to cottages and council houses, have a reputation for being haunted by those who once lived or died in them. The palatial mansion of Longleat in Wiltshire, for example, is haunted by a woman who appears in a passage at the top of the house, walking to and fro. She seems to be in an agony of fear and grief. Even when she is not visible, some people sense such an atmosphere of terror and misery in that passage that they cannot stay in it.

The ghostly figure is believed to be Lady Louisa Carteret, who married the second Lord Weymouth and died in 1736. Family tradition has it that the marriage was unhappy, that Lady Louisa took a lover and that her husband, returning home unexpectedly, caught them together. The husband and the lover fought with swords up and down the passage, watched by the horrified wife. Lord Weymouth killed the lover and secretly buried his body in the cellar.

Tradition is not always reliable, but in this case it is known that soon after the time when the duel is supposed to have been fought, Lord Weymouth left Longleat and refused ever to live there again; and some years ago, when central heating was being installed in the house, the remains of a young man in costume of the early eighteenth century were found under the cellar floor. No other incident in the history of the house accounts for this discovery.

OPPOSITE *Miss Annie Moberly and Miss Eleanor Jourdain on a visit to Versailles apparently saw various features of the gardens which had been there a century before but were not there in 1901.*

RIGHT *A view of Longleat House, near Warminster in Wiltshire, at about the time when Lady Louisa Carteret lived there.*

Mysterious Disappearances

The cases mentioned here constitute only a tiny fraction of those which have been reported. It is easy enough to dismiss any single case on the assumption that whoever reported it was either lying or imagining things, but the sheer quantity of evidence is impressive and much of it comes from people who do not seem at all fanciful. It seems clear that experiences of this kind do happen, whatever the explanation may be.

There are several tentative explanations. One is in terms of clairvoyance, the ability to become aware of events far distant in space and time, beyond the normal range of the senses. On this theory, a scene from the past, perceived clairvoyantly, is translated in the observer's mind into a perception of the visible figures of the actors and objects in the scene – projected, as it were, on to the screen of the outside world. Another theory is that, if an object may somehow retain an impression of a person who was closely associated with it, so may a place, so that people and episodes from the past may be seen there long afterwards. It is stretching this explanation rather far, however, to apply it to the eighteenth-century scenery of Versailles being seen in 1901, or to Roman legionaries being seen tramping along a stretch of Roman road.

Alternatively, perhaps the entire past is recorded somewhere in space-time, as if captured on film. Usually we see only the present, but occasionally a loop or warp or peculiarity of some sort occurs in time and part of the past is seen again as if a section of the film were being run through.

The same theory can be applied to reincarnation cases. Examples crop up every now and again of people claiming to remember previous lives and producing detailed information about the past, which on investigation proves strikingly accurate. Again, a possible explanation lies in unconscious clairvoyance, here translated into apparent memories of an earlier existence; but an alternative theory is that part of the past has been perceived as the result of a time-warp.

If oddities of time may possibly account for some mysterious happenings, perhaps others are a consequence of as yet unexplored peculiarities of space. There are numerous cases of people mysteriously disappearing and never being found again, alive or dead. In many cases, no doubt, the person who disappeared had every intention of doing so and took good care not to be found. In others – like that of the American writer Ambrose Bierce, who left New York in 1913, intending to go to Mexico, and disappeared into limbo – it is probably just a fluke that no trace was found.

Some of the cases, however, are distinctly strange. In 1880 a farmer named Lang suddenly vanished from the middle of a forty-acre field in Tennessee and was never seen again. Five people saw it happen, including Lang's two children, aged eleven and eight. Unless all five were in a conspiracy to conceal the truth – a conspiracy which resisted vigorous efforts to penetrate it – no one has ever been able to explain what happened.

In 1906, in England, the three children of the Vaughan family – a boy of ten and his two sisters, aged eight and seven – went to play in a field close to their home in Gloucester and did not come back. Police and neighbours searched the field and the surrounding area for three days without success.

Early in the morning of the fourth day the children were discovered fast asleep in a ditch at the edge of the field, although the ditch had been combed by the searchers. The children were unharmed and not particularly hungry; they did not know that three days had gone by and said they had no memory of what had happened to them after going into the field. The police were unable to find any satisfactory explanation and the obvious theory, that the children had been kidnapped and then returned, had to be dropped for lack of both evidence and motive. The boy in the case was interviewed many years later, when he was in his fifties, and still insisted that he had no recollection of what had happened during the missing three days.

What did happen to the Vaughan children? Were they either abducted or playing truant, and for some unknown reason lied about it ever afterwards? Were they, as some writers think, picked up by a passing flying saucer, fed and watered for three days and then returned to earth, their memories somehow erased? Did they fall into a warp in space-time? Is there a fifth dimension, into which people and things may mysteriously vanish?

The 'Mary Celeste'

The most famous of all mysterious disappearances is that of the crew of the *Mary Celeste*, an American sailing ship rumoured to be unlucky, which left New York harbour in November 1872, bound for Genoa with a small cargo of commercial alcohol. On board were Captain Benjamin Briggs, his wife and two-year-old daughter, and a crew of eight. None of them was seen again.

The *Mary Celeste* was followed across the Atlantic a few days later by a British sailing ship, the *Dei Gratia*, which left New York for Gibraltar. Captain David Moorhouse of the *Dei Gratia* was a friend

of Captain Briggs of the *Mary Celeste*. Early in December the *Dei Gratia* sighted the *Mary Celeste*, sails set but lurching about so erratically that Captain Moorhouse sent a party to investigate. There was not a soul on board her. The crew had apparently abandoned her, for her solitary lifeboat was missing, and so were the navigation instruments and ship's papers. There were signs that she had been abandoned in great haste, but nothing seemed to account for it. Although the vessel had suffered some storm damage, she was in no danger of sinking and there was plenty of food and water on board. The front hatch cover was off and one of the casks of alcohol was damaged, but the rest of the cargo was intact. Commercial alcohol is practically undrinkable and there was no evidence of a drunken quarrel or of a struggle of any kind. Two mysterious grooves were found on the *Mary Celeste*'s bows just above the waterline, and a mark on the ship's rail, apparently made by an axe. A prize crew from the *Dei Gratia* sailed the *Mary Celeste* to Gibraltar.

The story caused a furore. It was at first suggested that Captain Briggs and Captain Moorhouse had hatched a plot to collect the salvage money for the *Mary Celeste*. An alternative theory was that the men of the *Dei Gratia*, mistakenly believing that the *Mary Celeste* carried valuable cargo, seized her and killed everyone on board. The evidence was utterly inadequate to sustain either of these allegations. In later years

various 'survivors' of the *Mary Celeste* came forward with colourful stories of what had happened, but none of their names was on the ship's muster-roll.

It has been suggested that a whirl-wind, a giant sea-monster or a flying saucer snatched the whole crew clean off the ship – in which case it must have picked up the lifeboat, instruments and ship's papers as well! The simplest explanation is that during a storm those on board the *Mary Celeste* flew into a panic. Thinking she was about to sink, they hurried into the lifeboat, pulled away from her and were subsequently drowned. It is strange that experienced seamen should have reacted in terror to comparatively slight damage, but it is

ABOVE LEFT *Captain Benjamin Spooner Briggs, the master of the* Mary Celeste, *who vanished from the ship with his wife and two-year-old daughter, and the entire crew. The* Mary Celeste's *name had previously been changed, from* The Amazon, *and it is said that many sailors regarded her as an unlucky ship.*

ABOVE *Artist's impression of the party from the* Dei Gratia *rowing across to the* Mary Celeste, *which they found totally deserted. The disappearance without trace of all those on board created a sensation. The crew had apparently abandoned the ship in great haste, but nothing seemed to account for it.*

Ambrose Bierce, the sardonic American satirist and author of stories of the supernatural, left New York in 1913 for Mexico, at the age of seventy-one, and disappeared. However, Mexico was in the throes of a revolution at the time and it is probably a mere accident that no trace was ever found.

probably what happened. As a footnote to the story, the *Mary Celeste* herself came to an ignominious end: in 1885 she was deliberately wrecked and set on fire in an attempted insurance swindle.

An even more extraordinary story, but unfortunately not so well documented, is that of the *Ellen Austin*, a British sailing ship. Bound for St John's, Newfoundland, in 1881, she came across a drifting schooner in the Atlantic. A party from the *Ellen Austin* found her perfectly shipshape, but with no one on board; a prize crew stayed aboard her and the two ships sailed on together until a storm blew up. After the storm, men from the *Ellen Austin* rowed across to the schooner and found her completely deserted for the second time, with no sign of their shipmates. This discovery naturally created intense alarm on the *Ellen Austin*, but eventually four men agreed to sail the schooner to St John's. She drew ahead of the *Ellen Austin* and was lost to sight. She never reached St John's and was never heard of again.

ABOVE RIGHT *One of the last photographs taken of the* Star Tiger *of British South American Airways, which vanished entirely without trace in January 1948 within 400 miles of Bermuda. The same thing happened to a sister plane a year later.*

OPPOSITE *Some of the mysterious disappearances in the Bermuda Triangle:*
1 *Cyclops, 1918*
2 *La Dahana, 1935*
3 *Gloria Colita, 1940*
4 *Rubicon, 1944*
5 *Flight 19, 1945*
6 *Star Tiger, 1948*
7 *DC-3, 1948*
8 *Star Ariel, 1949*
9 *Southern Districts, 1954*
10 *Connemara IV, 1955*
11 *Revonoc, 1958*
12 *Marine Sulphur Queen, 1963*
13 *Two KC-135s, 1963*
14 *Piper Apache, 1967*

The Bermuda Triangle

Various ships and boats have been found drifting and empty in the notorious region of the Atlantic known as the Bermuda Triangle – the schooner *Gloria Colita* in 1940, for instance, and the freighter *Rubicon*, found with only a dog aboard in 1944. The Triangle owes its dubious fame, however, less to these incidents than to the numerous ships and aircraft which have set off into it and vanished, apparently into thin air. Planes and ships, some of substantial size, have disappeared without leaving wreckage, bodies, drifting lifeboats, oil-slicks, or debris behind them, as if they had flown or sailed straight into a different dimension.

The Triangle, strictly speaking, is the area of the Atlantic between the Florida coast of the United States, Bermuda and Puerto Rico. Many authors, how-

ever, have extended the area and given it a more rectangular shape. The fact that the area includes the Sargasso Sea, where the ocean is covered with floating seaweed, which was long believed to trap ships and hold them fast, has added to the Triangle's sinister aura.

In 1918, for example, the American Navy cargo ship *Cyclops*, with 300 people on board, was lost without trace in a vanishing act which the US Navy described as a baffling mystery. In 1963 a tanker of 7,000 tons, the *Marine Sulphur Queen*, disappeared with her crew of 39, and all that rescue boats and planes could find was a lifebelt, a lifejacket and a man's shirt. The 20,000-ton coal-freighter *Anita*, with a crew of 32, vanished without any trace at all in 1973.

In January 1948 a British South American Airways plane, *Star Tiger*, a converted Lancaster bomber, carrying 31 passengers and crew, was flying from the Azores to Bermuda. When the plane was less than 400 miles from Bermuda

the pilot radioed that the weather was fine and the performance of the aircraft excellent and he expected to land on time. The *Star Tiger* never arrived and a massive search operation failed to find any trace of her whatever. The same thing happened a year later to a sister plane, the *Star Ariel*, which disappeared on her way from Bermuda to Jamaica in calm weather and sea conditions. Courts of enquiry into both losses were baffled.

The incident which began the whole Bermuda Triangle uproar occurred in December 1945 when US Navy Flight 19, consisting of five Grumman Avenger torpedo-bombers, set off on a routine training mission from their base at Fort Lauderdale, Florida, and disappeared from the sky above the Atlantic to the east of the Bahamas. An intensive rescue effort found no trace of the planes, and one of the search aircraft itself vanished, a bulky Martin Mariner seaplane with a crew of 13.

The control tower at Fort Lauderdale was at first in touch with the

Avenger bombers by radio, and messages showed the pilots becoming hopelessly confused. They did not know where they were or which way they were heading because their compasses and navigation instruments had gone wild, for no reason anyone was afterwards able to pin down. Where they expected to see land there was none, and one pilot made the mysterious comment that the sea did not look as it should. Heavy static made communication increasingly difficult, until the tower finally lost contact with the planes altogether. An official board of enquiry into the disaster was at a loss to explain what had happened.

There have been other (though far fewer) reports of ships vanishing into thin air in the so-called Devil's Sea, in the Pacific south-east of Japan. In 1955 a party of scientists took a ship to the area to investigate; the ship disappeared, and the scientists with it.

The first problem about the Bermuda Triangle (and the Devil's Sea) is whether any great mystery really exists

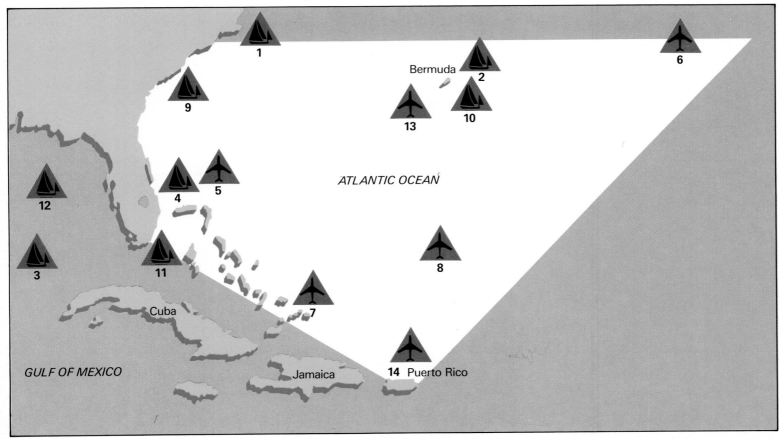

after all. Ships and planes *can* sink and leave no trace without factors unknown to science being involved. The Triangle is extremely heavily travelled, by sea and air, and the question is whether 100 to 150 cases of unaccountable disappearance in the area are unduly surprising. Many people think not, and according to figures issued by the US Coast Guard, disappearances in the Triangle are no more frequent, in relation to the amount of traffic, than elsewhere.

The second problem is that there are far too many tentative explanations of the disappearances. They range from sudden storms, structural failures, fireballs or undersea earthquakes to insurance swindles or piracy, and on to space-time warps, attacking sea-monsters, marauding UFOs collecting human specimens, or Atlantean lasers of colossal power deep in the sea. It is not possible to find a path through this jungle of explanations with any confidence. This applies to the more orthodox theories as well as to the wilder ones, which is why official enquiries have again and again proved inconclusive. A disappearance without trace is usually impossible to explain, precisely because the evidence which might explain it is missing.

One curious phenomenon, however, is the number of reports of unexplained failure of electrical and mechanical equipment in the Triangle. The case of Flight 19 is the most dramatic, but in 1975 the radio transmitter and navigation gear of a US Coast Guard cutter broke down completely, for no ascertainable reason. At the same time, according to the crew, strange green lights were falling from the sky. The year before, in another Coast Guard cutter, the radio went wrong and a large landmass loomed up on the radar screen where no land was, but no one could find any fault in the radar equipment. The Coast Guard is not given to issuing fanciful reports and is among the sternest opponents of the Bermuda Triangle 'mystery'. Quite a number of similar puzzling incidents have been reported since the 1940s and there seems to be a genuine mystery here, awaiting explanation.

BELOW *The United States Navy cargo ship* Cyclops, *which disappeared on her way to Baltimore in March 1918, with more than three hundred people on board. Leaving Barbados, where she had coaled, the* Cyclops *vanished without sending out a distress signal and without leaving wreckage or any other trace.*

Bursting into Flames

An even more lethal phenomenon, not yet explained, is 'spontaneous human combustion', when a person suddenly bursts into flames, for no evident cause and with an astonishing intensity of heat. The most celebrated modern case occurred in 1966 in Coudersport, Pennsylvania. A meter-reader went into the house of a retired doctor in his nineties, John Irving Bentley, and noticed a strange smell and peculiar light-blue smoke. Investigating, he found a blackened hole in the floor of the bathroom. Beside it were Dr Bentley's steel walking-frame and the lower part of his right leg, burned brown and with the shoe still on. All the rest that was left of the unfortunate doctor proved to be in the basement, below the hole in the bathroom floor – a knee-joint and a pile of ash.

The suggestion that Dr Bentley had set fire to himself while lighting his pipe did not fit the evidence, nor did it explain how a fire of such fierceness had failed to do far more damage to the house. The bathtub, for example, which was near the hole in the floor, was not badly scorched, though the heat must have been intense.

This curiously limited, local effect of the combustion has occurred in other cases. How spontaneous human combustion begins is not understood, nor how the human body in flames can generate the high temperatures required to reduce the tissues and bones to ash. The occasional cases reported are among the weirdest of unexplained occurrences.

ABOVE RIGHT *Officials inspecting the debris in the house where Mrs Mary Reeser died, in St Petersburg, Florida, on 2 July 1951. She apparently burst spontaneously into flames while sitting in her armchair and burned with such intensity that her skull shrank to the size of an orange.*

RIGHT *The lower right leg of Dr John Irving Bentley of Coudersport, Pennsylvania, who apparently perished by spontaneous combustion on 5 December 1966. The unfortunate doctor's steel walking aid can be seen. It is not known how a fire of such fierceness failed to do far more damage to the bathroom.*

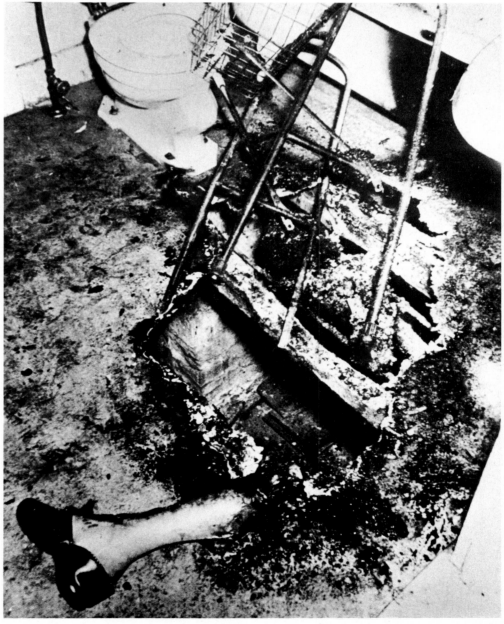

Out of the Blue

While some people suddenly and inexplicably catch fire, and others mysteriously disappear, there are also reports of things equally mysteriously appearing out of the blue. An eccentric American journalist named Charles Fort spent years of his life (he died in 1932) rummaging through newspapers and scientific periodicals for accounts of extraordinary happenings. From his dusty explorations in the files of the New York Public Library and the British Museum he brought back astonishing trophies, which he called 'the damned', meaning 'the data that Science has excluded'. Among them were reports of remarkable coincidences, poltergeist phenomena and strange things seen in the sky – some of which resemble more recent descriptions of UFOs. There were also accounts of all sorts of things suddenly and startlingly falling out of the sky, including frogs, toads, fishes, ice, jelly, salt, coal, ants, worms, pebbles, stone balls, snakes, snails, mussels and lizards.

As so often with mysterious events, no single example is particularly impressive by itself. It is the sheer weight of them that tells. In 1876 flakes of a substance that looked like beef fell out of a clear blue sky at Olympian Springs, Kentucky. The flakes were two or three inches square. One analyst said the substance was lung tissue. After torrential rain at Memphis, Tennessee, in 1877, in two city blocks, and only in those blocks, legions of snakes were found crawling on the ground, though no one had seen them fall. In 1911 in England, at Eton in Buckinghamshire, after heavy rain, the ground was covered with masses of jelly, the size of peas. The jelly contained numerous eggs of some species of insect, from which larvae soon emerged. Hundreds of mussels fell out of a yellow cloud which appeared over Paderborn in Germany in 1892. In Wales in 1859 thousands of live sticklebacks fell from the sky at a place called Mountain Ash in Glamorgan. Some of them landed on the ground and some on the roofs of houses; there were two falls, ten minutes

apart. Some of the fish were taken to the London Zoo in Regent's Park, where they thrived.

The obvious explanation of falls of fish, frogs and similar creatures is that they have been sucked up from the land, a pond, a river, or the sea by a whirlwind, carried some distance and then deposited again. Perhaps this is the right answer in some cases, but it is not easy to accept in others. For one thing, no whirlwind is usually reported. For another, as Fort pointed out, it is a strange whirlwind which drops frogs or fish or insects, but refrains from dropping fragments of pondweed, leaves, twigs and other debris.

Fort remarked of cases of this kind (in *The Book of the Damned*):

I think of a region somewhere above this earth's surface in which gravitation is inoperative . . . I think that things raised from this earth's surface to that region have been held there until shaken down by storms –
The Super-Sargasso Sea.
Derelicts, rubbish, old cargoes from interplanetary wrecks; things cast out into what is called space by convulsions of other planets, things from the times of the Alexanders, Caesars and Napoleons of

Mars and Jupiter and Neptune; things raised by this earth's cyclones: horses and barns and elephants and flies, dodos, moas and pterodactyls . . .

Whether Fort seriously thought there was a Sargasso Sea of flotsam in the sky, and civilizations on Mars, Jupiter and Neptune, is not clear. He lived before the age of space travel, but in any case he had a sardonic sense of humour and delighted in throwing out such suggestions as that human beings are the cattle of some super-terrestrial farmer. In the end he had no general theory to account for the extraordinary events he collected. 'Here are the data,' he said. 'Make what you will, yourself, of them.'

OPPOSITE *Accounts of things falling inexplicably from the sky go back for centuries. The Bible (Exodus, chapter 16) describes how bread or 'manna' rained miraculously on the Israelites when they were in the wilderness of Sinai. They are shown gathering the manna in this fifteenth-century Flemish painting.*

ABOVE *The cover of* Lo! *(1931), one of Charles Fort's books, showing a rain of frogs falling from the sky. Reports of things appearing mysteriously out of the blue were among the peculiar unexplained phenomena which fascinated Fort and encouraged him in his sardonic contempt for conventional science.*

Frogs, Seeds and Poltergeists

What to make of them is puzzling, but Fortean phenomena have not ceased since Fort's time, far from it. In 1948 a downpour of herrings landed on a golf course at Bournemouth in England. During a heavy storm in Birmingham in 1954 hundreds of small frogs fell out of the sky, bouncing off umbrellas and raincoats. In 1973 thousands of small toads fell from the sky at Brignoles in the south of France. In 1977 a couple out walking in Bristol, England, were caught in a shower of hazelnuts, 300 or more of them. There were no nut trees in the road and the nuts were fresh and tasty, although this happened in March and hazelnuts do not ripen until the autumn. One day in 1979 showers of mustard and cress seeds, encased in sticky jelly, fell five or six times on a house in a suburb of Southampton. The

following day seeds of peas and beans fell in the garden, and also in the next-door garden; the owner of the house on the other side opened her front door and was hit by a fusillade of broad bean seeds. Only these three houses in the street were affected: the police were called in but could make nothing of it. The seeds were planted and grew normally.

One tentative line of explanation is a fifth dimension, from which things suddenly appear. Another is suggested by the gradual accumulation of evidence for 'psychokinesis', the human mind's ability to exert a direct influence on matter. Is it possible that a person on the scene unconsciously causes a fall of frogs, seeds, or whatever it may be?

The idea seems distinctly far-fetched, but evidence of the mind's power to cause objects to move about comes from parapsychology laboratories and from poltergeist cases. These are cases in which disturbances begin in a house. Inexplicable knocks and bangings are

heard, pieces of furniture move about by themselves, ornaments and dishes fly off tables and shelves and smash on the floor. In the old days they were put down to a poltergeist or 'noisy spirit', a demon infesting the house. Quite a number of recent cases have been carefully investigated without any sign of deliberate trickery, and they are now attributed to unconscious human agency. It seems that someone in the house in a deeply disturbed state of mind, often an adolescent, is unconsciously causing the disturbances by psychokinesis.

In a labourer's house at Nickelheim, Germany, in 1968, mysterious knocks on doors and windows were heard, objects flew about and stones unaccountably penetrated into closed rooms. On one occasion, when a priest was inside blessing the house, a stone fell from the ceiling although all the doors and windows were shut. The case was investigated by a leading parapsychologist, Professor Hans Bender of Freiburg

Human Teleportation

There are occasional reports of human beings mysteriously disappearing from one place and reappearing in another. In 1968, for instance, a doctor and his wife were driving along a road in Argentina when their car entered a thick bank of mist. The next they knew, they were on a road near Mexico City, thousands of miles away; they had lost two days in between, of which they had no recollection.

The most famous case of teleportation – in the West at least – is that of a celebrated mystic of the seventeenth century, Sister Mary of Agreda, a Spanish nun who claimed that she had frequently 'flown' from Spain to America to teach the Indians about Christianity. She was at first assumed to be talking hysterical nonsense, but meantime the Jumano Indians in New Mexico were telling missionaries that a mysterious lady in a blue habit – the uniform of Sister Mary's order – had often visited them and preached to them. Later, one of the missionaries returned to Spain, interviewed Sister Mary at length and became convinced, from her detailed knowledge of the Indians, that the story was true. Others were not convinced, and at this late date it is impossible to be sure of the evidence

University: in one test, some bottles were placed on the kitchen table and everyone went outside, with the house being closed up tight. Soon afterwards the bottles appeared outside the house, at roof level, and fell to the ground. Professor Bender traced these extraordinary occurrences to a thirteen-year-old girl in the house, who was in a disturbed state and appeared to be causing them unconsciously. There is possibly a parallel between the falling bottles in this case and falling frogs, toads and the rest.

ABOVE '*Raining Cats, Dogs and Pitchforks*' by *George Cruikshank, nineteenth century. Frogs and fishes are among the most commonly reported falls. Thousands of small frogs rained on a house in Buckinghamshire in 1969 and thousands more fell in the desert in Morocco in 1977.*

RIGHT *In 1955 a French reporter and photographer went to a house infested by a poltergeist at St Jean de Maurienne, occupied by the Costa family. This photograph shows Mrs Costa holding her baby while a saucepan, its lid, a pair of scissors and a telegraph form fly through the air.*

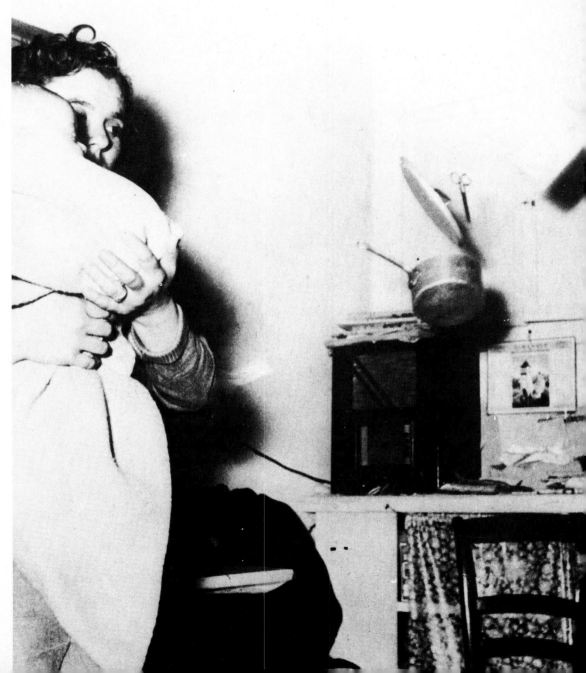

Intruders and Monsters

Intruders and Monsters

The ability to move from one place to another a great distance away without the use of any of the normal means of transport has been credited to holy men and women, shamans and magicians, all over the world. Perhaps there is more to this old and widespread belief than meets the eye, but not all cases of the kind, as described by those who experience them, are examples of teleportation. There are other reports in which Unidentified Flying Objects are involved.

In 1961, for example, an American couple named Hill were driving at night when they saw a bright object in the sky. They began to feel sleepy; an hour later they woke up, still in the car but thirty-five miles away, with no recollection of how they had got there. The Hills were eventually hypnotized, separately, and under hypnosis their stories agreed: the bright object was a UFO, with light streaming from portholes in its sides; the Hills were taken on board the UFO by its crew, who were small man-like creatures, and were medically examined; they were then put back in their car further along the road, and their conscious minds were wiped clear of the memory of what had happened.

Evidence given under hypnosis, unfortunately, is not necessarily less contaminated by fantasy than evidence which is not given under hypnosis. It is also questionable, because hypnotized subjects become abnormally suggestible and responsive, not merely to leading questions but to the slightest hint of what they think the questioner expects or wants them to say.

There are, however, innumerable other reports of UFOs, including some from people who claim to have encountered them at close quarters. A Gallup poll in 1974 showed that one American in every ten had seen a UFO, and this figure made no allowance for people too embarrassed to make the claim.

OPPOSITE *A 'flying saucer'. The earliest reports of UFOs came from the United States in 1947.*

PREVIOUS PAGES *The Loch Ness monster, photographed by Anthony Shiels in May 1977.*

Close Encounters of Three Kinds

Professor J. Allen Hynek, an American astronomer who is Director of the Centre for UFO Studies, has classified UFO experiences in two main categories. Most of them are 'distant' experiences, when the mysterious object is seen more than 500 feet (150 m) away. The less common category, of close encounters, is subdivided into three. A 'close encounter of the first kind' is a simple observation of the object at a range of less than 500 feet. In a 'close encounter of the second kind' physical effects are observed as well, such as flattened or scorched vegetation, marks made by the UFO on the ground, or failure of car engines or radios. 'Close encounters of the third kind' are those in which occupants of the UFO are seen.

The occupants are often described as 'humanoid' or human-like. A French farmer, who claimed to have seen two of the crew of a UFO in 1965, said they were small man-like creatures with large heads, slanting eyes, thin mouths, puffy cheeks and pointed chins. Similar features were reported by the Hills.

Some people claim to have spoken with beings from UFOs, but Professor Hynek dismisses all reports of this kind on the ground that they invariably come from witnesses of inadequate credibility, and frequently from witnesses who have some sort of pseudo-religious axe to grind. This is the type of case in which someone claims to have been carried off to Mars or Venus or an unknown planet in a UFO. There he meets beneficent and all-wise beings, who send him back to earth, charged with the message that humanity must mend its evil ways and take to universal love and brotherhood, or face destruction. The activities of these 'contactees', as they are called, are not always noticeably benevolent. In 1968, after a wave of bomb outrages in Brazil, a man who had earlier published a book about his meetings with space beings was arrested as a terrorist. At his trial he claimed to be a Venusian agent, preparing the way for an armada of UFOs which would soon invade and conquer the earth.

Cases like this add fuel to the fires of the sceptics, who put all UFO experiences down to fantasy, deliberate lying, or, more often than not, mistaken observation. There is no doubt that the sceptics are frequently right. Some reports of UFOs have turned out to be hoaxes; many more have been convincingly explained as sightings of aircraft, rockets, space satellites, weather balloons, clouds, swarms of insects lit up by St Elmo's Fire, planets – especially Venus – and other perfectly identifiable airborne objects, which have been sincerely but erroneously taken for UFOs. Which is just as well, because it has been calculated that if all the reports were well-founded, UFOs must have made landfall on the earth something like three million times in the last twenty-five years.

Whether the sceptics have succeeded in explaining all the sightings away is open to question. The situation is quite different from that of mysterious disappearances in the Bermuda Triangle, where eyewitness evidence is inevitably conspicuous by its absence. UFOs have been seen by numerous level-headed witnesses whose evidence about anything else would command respect, including experienced pilots, engineers and technicians familiar with aircraft, clouds, planets and other recognized phenomena of the sky. It is quite often possible to check whether Venus, or a space satellite or whatever, was or was not visible at the time and place of a sighting; and yet no convincing 'normal' explanation has been found for some of the experiences. A report issued by the US Air Force in 1969 left about one in three of its eighty-seven case-histories unexplained, and stonewalling by the scientific and military authorities has caused the sceptical position itself to be viewed with some cynicism. The Air Force's own investigatory project became known as 'the Society for the Explanation of the Uninvestigated'.

UFOs are not the only apparently alien or extraordinary intruders into our world. There are less frequent but persistent reports of strange monsters and humanoids, of mysterious footprints and other traces of creatures which ought not to exist. Again, though most of these reports are probably false, hysterical or mistaken, some are not easy to explain away. It seems that people do on occasion see things which are not readily accounted for.

This raises the perplexing question of what kind of reality is involved. Are UFOs and other intruders creations of the human mind? Does a deep need for mysterious 'visitors' somehow call them into existence? Or do UFOs and other unexplained visitors exist independently in their own right? Are there more beings and creatures in the world with us than we know?

The Flying Saucer Phenomenon

The term 'flying saucer' originated with the curious experience of an American pilot named Kenneth Arnold in 1947. He was flying near Mount Rainier in Washington State, when he saw nine objects in the sky, flying in two files. They appeared to be metallic discs, silvery on top and black underneath. He estimated that they measured about 100 feet across and were travelling at a minimum of 1,200 miles per hour, or about twice the speed which had at that time been achieved by aircraft. They flew in an odd way, dipping, fluttering and sailing, which he described at a press conference as like a saucer skipping across water. The 'flying saucer' was promptly born in the newspaper headlines.

The name is misleading, because UFOs have been seen in an astonishing variety of shapes: cylindrical, cigar-shaped, oval, globular, conical, domed like an upturned soup plate, domed and colonnaded, double-domed like one soup plate upside down on another, in the shape of a doughnut, a tadpole, or even a giant light bulb. They have also been reported in widely differing sizes,

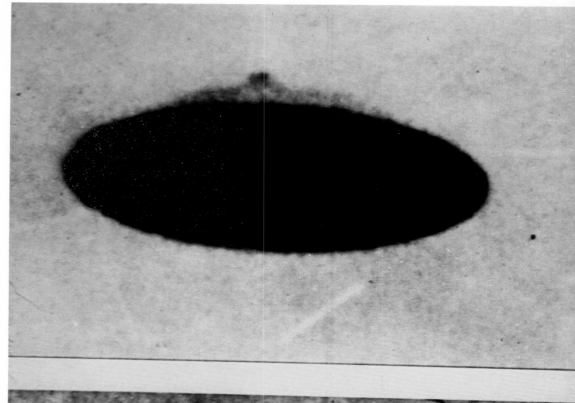

and these variations have contributed to scepticism about them.

In 1954 the captain and crew, and fourteen out of fifty-one passengers, reported seeing UFOs from an airliner flying over the Atlantic off Labrador. Mysterious objects showed up on ground control radar at the same time, and also on the radar of a Sabre jet fighter which was sent up to investigate. From the airliner, a large object was seen emerging from a gap in the clouds.

Manoeuvring about it were six smaller objects, apparently daughter-ships. They formed into single file on the approach of the Sabre jet and merged into one end of the principal object, which then shrank in size and disappeared. The captain of the airliner reported that the large object, when he first saw it, kept changing shape. At one moment it looked like a delta wing, at another like a telephone handset, at another like a large pear. What are we to make of this? The mind boggles.

A more typical sighting occurred at the end of 1978, when an Australian television film crew, flying at night to Wellington, New Zealand, saw mysterious lights in the sky. This was reported to Wellington ground control, which confirmed that unidentified objects had been picked up on radar. Later, on the return journey, an object described as having a transparent dome and a brightly lit base appeared to one side of the plane. When the pilot flew towards it, it kept its distance for a time and then suddenly shot across the plane's bows and disappeared below it. Suggestions that what had been seen was Venus or another planet or the lights of a fishing fleet reflected in the sky were checked, and it was found that Venus was not visible at the time, the other planets were not in the right positions, and the fishing fleet was too far away. No other conventional explanation was found to fit the circumstances either.

In these two cases, unless all concerned were collaborating in a hoax, the phenomenon was seen by several people, and was also observed on radar. Both these factors militate against the sceptical dismissal of UFOs and also – at first sight at least – against the theory that they are creations of the mind.

Photographs ought to settle the reality of UFOs once and for all, but unfortunately they do not. Not only are the great majority of UFO photographs generally agreed to be faked, including all the best ones, but the camera can lie all too readily, even without the assistance of the photographer. The less suspect photographs are so vague and blurred that they provide no proof of anything, and raise the question whether, if UFOs do exist, they are for some reason resistant to photography. Or if they are creations of the mind, perhaps mental creations do not show up well on film (like ghosts?).

However, there are reports of UFOs leaving more tangible evidence behind them than blurred photographs. In 1964, at Socorro, New Mexico, a policeman on patrol in his car saw a

OPPOSITE ABOVE *UFO photographed over Trinidade Island off the South American coast in January 1958. UFOs are usually assumed to come from an advanced civilization in outer space, despite the problem of the immense distances which spacecraft from distant star-systems would have to travel.*

OPPOSITE CENTRE *UFO photographed in 1954 by an Australian rancher. The fact that UFOs have been reported in a bewildering variety of shapes and sizes has added fuel to the fires of scepticism about them. Many claimed sightings are undoubtedly mistaken or imaginary.*

OPPOSITE BELOW *These three UFOs were photographed over Conisbrough in Yorkshire by Stephen Pratt in March 1966.*

BELOW *UFO photographed at Merlin, Oregon, in 1964. The object bears an all too close and obvious resemblance to a lighting fixture. Whatever the truth about this photograph may be, there is no doubt that the camera can readily lie, as the fake 'UFO' (top), photographed from a television screen, demonstrates.*

light or flame descending from the sky some distance away. He drove over rough ground to the scene, where he saw, less than 200 yards (185 m) away, an oval, shiny, metallic object standing on girder-like legs. Close to it were two small man-like figures, about four feet tall, in white, astronaut-type clothing. He got out of his car and walked towards the object. There were thumping noises and then a loud roar, rising in pitch. The two figures were no longer visible, but he saw the object rising from the ground, with a blue and orange flame. It climbed gradually higher and flew away.

When another policeman arrived to help, the brush where the object had stood was still burning and there were four depressions in the ground, apparently made by the legs of the UFO's landing gear. An engineer inspected the marks and reported that they were consistent with the gentle settling of a weight of at least a ton on each mark. Four other, small round marks were found, which were described as footprints. This is one of the cases for which neither the US Air Force nor Professor Hynek could find any satisfactory conventional explanation.

Visitors from Space?

UFOs are usually assumed to come from outer space, from a civilization or civilizations considerably more advanced technologically than our own. They are crewed by space-beings, who are either humanoid in appearance or are able to adopt a humanoid disguise. They come here, according to various theories, to investigate our planet and its inhabitants, to collect specimens, to spy out the land for invasion and colonization, to watch over the progress of mankind, or to keep a eye on their human flocks and herds.

Unfortunately, none of the people who claim to have been on board a

UFO has ever brought back as a souvenir an object not manufactured on earth, nor has any UFO ever left such an object behind it. There is also the problem of the enormous distances involved. The nearest star-system which might have life in it is Alpha Centauri, and even if spacecraft from that system had a speed of seventy million miles per hour, it would still take them almost a hundred years to fly to the earth and back again. This would seem a formidable undertaking, and for any civilization further away the journey would be more daunting still.

An alternative theory is that UFOs do not come from outer space, but from a different dimension altogether, outside our space-time. This would explain why they suddenly appear out of nowhere and disappear into nowhere again. On this view, UFOs belong to a sphere of existence beyond our comprehension, and arguments about them in terms of our scientific system may well be meaningless.

Or is it possible that UFOs belong not to outer space but to *inner* space, as creations of the human mind? Their variations of shape suggest this but, if so, they must be mental creations of convincing solidity, because they are sometimes seen by several people at once, they show up on radar and they sometimes leave tangible evidence behind them – like the marks on the ground at Socorro. We know that the mind can play strange tricks. It can certainly impose convincing hallucinations on its owner and, the evidence suggests, it can directly influence matter: can it impose hallucinations on other people's minds as well, and imprint them on the material world? One suggestion is that mankind has a profound religious need for saviour-figures, for a supernatural source of spiritual security. In response to this need, and with the decline of the established religions, humanity has projected UFOs on to the outside world as vehicles of great saving beings in the sky, and projected them with such force that they actually materialize.

Were the Gods Astronauts?

Once interest in flying saucers had been aroused, it did not take long for writers to point out that records of people seeing strange, unexplained things in the sky stretch back for centuries. Were these reports really sightings of UFOs, and might beings from outside our world have visited the earth many thousands of years ago? If so, as products of a highly advanced civilization, might they have had a dominating influence on human history? This enticing avenue of speculation led to the now widely popular theory that long ago in the remote past superhuman beings came to the earth, created the human race in their own image (as God is described doing in the Bible) and laid the foundations of our civilization. It was their superior wisdom and technology which made possible the building of the pyramids, the construction of the prehistoric stone circles and all the other achievements of early man.

The best-known exponent of this belief is the Swiss writer Erich von Däniken. His first book, *Chariots of the Gods?*, was originally published in 1968, in German (under the evocative title *Erinnerungen an die Zukunft*, 'Memories of the Future'). Von Däniken's books have sold in millions of copies in innumerable languages, their appeal unaffected by the fact that his theories have been repeatedly torn to shreds and exposed as a tissue of false claims and misunderstood evidence.

Years before von Däniken entered the lists, it had been suggested that the gods of Egypt, Mesopotamia, Greece and Rome – immensely powerful, all-knowing superhuman beings, believed to live in the sky – were originally space-travellers, whose visits to the earth so impressed ignorant and brutish humanity that they were worshipped as gods. Ancient myths from all over the world, it was argued, told of the coming of powerful and wise civilization-bringers from the sky, and just beneath the surface of the Bible lay concealed the true early history of mankind.

In the opening chapter of Genesis, describing the creation of the world, God says, 'Let us make man.' Why *us*? Who were the other beings involved? The conventional answer is that God was speaking to the angels of his heavenly court. Space-fantasists, however, maintain that the makers of man were superbeings from the distant reaches of the galaxy, of whom 'God' was one. Brinsley le Poer Trench, for example, in his book *The Sky People*, suggested that man did not originate on earth at all, but was brought here by extraterrestrial astronauts, the 'sky people'. Man was created on the planet Mars – the Garden of Eden in the Bible – by 'God' (Jehovah) who was one of the sky people. Later, Jehovah was expelled from Mars and came to earth in a spaceship, bringing some human beings with him. In the Bible this has turned into the story of Noah and the Ark, but Noah was really Jehovah and the Ark was the spaceship.

The destruction of Sodom and Gomorrah was a nuclear explosion, which the sky people set off (it is conventionally explained as probably the result of an earthquake). The Ten Commandments were given to Moses by Jehovah, who landed on Mount Sinai in a spaceship. The Bible's description (in Exodus, chapter 20) of God descending on Mount Sinai in fire, with thunder rumbling and lightning flashing from a thick cloud of smoke, while the mountain quaked and the people trembled with fear, is explained as the reaction of ignorant and awe-struck human beings to the descent of a spacecraft.

Von Däniken agreed about Sodom and Gomorrah, but provided a different version of the origin of mankind. He fastened on the story (in Genesis, chapter 6) that the 'sons of God', or angels, married the 'daughters of men' and had children by them, 'mighty men which were of old, men of renown.' Long ago, von Däniken thought, a spaceship discovered earth and found that it was suited to the development of

intelligent life. The earth was inhabited at that time by an inferior, ape-like species (Neanderthal man, presumably). The spacemen or 'sons of God' artificially fertilized some of the females, the 'daughters of men', and so created *homo sapiens* in an experiment in selective breeding.

Speculation of this kind is fascinating because it brings old myths to life again in new patterns of meaning, but it rests on no evidence whatever. We do not even know that space-travellers from other worlds exist, let alone that they have ever visited the earth. With a little ingenuity, it is easy enough to remould carefully chosen Bible stories and ancient myths like plasticine into any shape required. This objection has not prevented astronaut-fantasists from fondly imagining that when the Bible says that Elijah was carried up into the sky in a fiery chariot drawn by fiery horses (II Kings, chapter 2), the 'chariot' must have been a spacecraft, though it would be more sensible to wonder whether the story has any basis in reality at all.

Ezekiel's vision of the chariot of God is another favourite of astronaut-fantasy. The prophet gives a long and extremely confused description (Ezekiel, chapter 1) of seeing a whirl-wind coming out of the north, with fire and a cloud and four manlike creatures, shining like brass or glowing coals. Each had straight feet, four wings and four faces – of a man, a lion, an ox and an eagle. He also saw wheels, and a wheel in the middle of a wheel, and rings full of eyes. Obviously, we are told, Ezekiel saw space-beings and a kind of space-helicopter. The context, however, makes it clear that he is trying to describe a vision, something not seen with the normal eye but in an unusual state of consciousness. The winged creatures with four faces are probably based on the figures of the cherubim which stood in the Holy of Holies, the dwelling-place of God in the Temple at Jerusalem. If the vision is taken literally, for no good reason, we are forced to wonder whether visiting astronauts really have four faces, four wings and flat feet.

Another favourite theory is that Jesus was a spaceman and the Star of Bethlehem, which the Three Wise Men followed, was a spaceship. The likelihood is that it was either a conjunction of Saturn and Jupiter in the year 7 BC or a nova (a previously unknown star which flares up brightly as if it had suddenly sprung to life). For the fantasists, however, Jesus was brought to earth in a spaceship, or alternatively he was fathered on Mary by a superbeing from space, not sexually but by mental power, and after his death and resurrection he was taken away in a spacecraft. If this is what happened, one wonders why the New Testament does not describe Jesus being carried up into the sky in a 'fiery chariot', in the style of Elijah and Ezekiel.

It is often claimed that various supposedly mysterious objects on the earth are evidence of visiting astronauts in the past, but the claims fail to hold water. It was argued, for instance, that the massive statues on Easter Island could not be the work of the natives of the island, who were far too backward, and must have been erected by space-men. This theory was exploded in 1956, when the islanders carved and erected a new statue successfully, using only their traditional methods and without extra-terrestrial assistance. Or there is the 'astronaut' of a temple at Palenque in Mexico, where a stone grave-slab is supposed to represent a helmeted space-man at the controls of a rocket. The slab, which dates from the seventh century AD, in fact shows a Mayan king with a sacred maize plant. The carving is entirely explainable in the context of traditional Mayan art: there is nothing mysterious about it and it has nothing to do with spacemen or rockets. The Nazca desert lines in Peru are genuinely mysterious but, whatever their expla-nation may be, they were not laid out to help visiting astronauts land their spaceships, because the ground is far too soft to make a viable airfield.

The astronaut-fantasy is really an attempt to explain the conflict between the evidence that man, thousands of years ago, possessed remarkably ad-vanced scientific knowledge, and the evidence that in other ways ancient societies were primitive and backward by modern standards. The fantasy answer is that visitors from a far more advanced civilization supplied the knowledge which enabled the Egypt-ians to build the Great Pyramid and the megalithic architects to construct Stonehenge. It is a return to the now discredited belief that the further back into the past history goes, the more savage, ignorant and stupid human beings must have been. Our ancestors could not have built the pyramids and laid out the stone circles unaided, so the theory runs, because they were too barbarous to do so. This turned out not to be true of the Easter Islanders, and is almost certainly not true of the ancient world either.

The most interesting thing about the theory of visiting astronauts creating our civilization is its popularity. Mill-ions of people have evidently found it fascinating and satisfying. The prin-cipal factor in this response may be that

the astronaut-theory supplies god-substitutes. The gods of the ancient world are dead, and belief in the major modern religions has been ebbing away. The gap is filled by surpassingly power-ful beings from outside our world, in a fantasy well suited to the space age and based on a need for superhuman figures, stronger and wiser than ourselves.

The stone grave-slab of the Mayan King Pacal shows him seated on a throne in front of a symbol of rebirth, a cross-shaped maize plant. According to von Däniken Pacal is an astronaut who is 'manipulating a number of unidentifiable controls and has the heel of his left foot on a kind of pedal.'

SMYTH   WEEDON OY

Sea Monsters

Whether or not there are alien beings in our skies, it is highly likely that there are unknown creatures in the sea. Two-thirds of the earth's surface is covered by water, in some places to a depth of 6 miles (9.5 km). Most of this vast area is still unexplored, some of its denizens have only recently been recognized by science, and many others probably remain to be recognized. The massive megamouth shark, for example, was not discovered until 1976, when one was accidentally hauled up from the ocean by a US Navy ship. The existence of highly poisonous sea snakes in the Pacific, though frequently reported by the local fishermen, was not scientifically confirmed until the 1940s.

Other sea creatures of popular belief, at one time contemptuously dismissed as old wives' tales, may well be real. A case in point is the Kraken, stories about which were collected in the eighteenth century by a Norwegian bishop, Erik Pontoppidan. Seen frequently off the

coast of Norway, it was said to seize ships, dragging them under with its many arms, and was at least a mile and a half in circumference. The legendary Kraken can now be identified as an exaggerated picture of the giant squid. These creatures do indeed have numerous arms and some of them are extremely large: one which was 60 feet (18 m) long was washed ashore in Newfoundland in 1878; another of similar size was observed by the USS *San Pablo* off Newfoundland in 1966; and one said to be more than 175 feet (53 m) in length was seen from a ship in the Indian Ocean during the Second World War. It is also known that giant squids do sometimes grapple with ships and even sink them: a tanker of 15,000 tons, the *Brunswick*, was attacked by one in the 1930s; and in the nineteenth century, in the Bay of Bengal, the 150-ton schooner *Pearl* was seized and capsized by a giant squid.

So far, no totally unchallengeable evidence has been obtained of the giant sea serpents which have frequently been reported. Sailors and fishermen have a

The sea serpent observed by HMS Daedalus *in the Atlantic, on her way from the Cape of Good Hope to St Helena, in 1848: artist's impression, in the* Illustrated London News, *based on the captain's description of the creature in his report to the Admiralty.*

reputation for spinning tall tales to landsmen, but so many reports have come from apparently reliable witnesses in the last 150 years that it takes a determined sceptic to write them all off. In 1848, for example, the captain of the British frigate *Daedalus*, with his professional reputation at stake, reported to the Admiralty that in the South Atlantic he and his officers and crew had seen 'a sea serpent of extraordinary dimensions', which they had watched for about twenty minutes. At least 60 feet (18 m) of it was visible and it held its snake-like head four feet or so above the water. It was dark brown in colour, with yellowish-white at the throat. It had no fins, but something like a bunch of seaweed or a horse's mane washed about its back.

In 1915 a German submarine torpedoed a British steamer in the North Atlantic. The steamer sank, watched from the U-boat's conning tower by the German captain and some of his crew. A few seconds later there was a violent explosion under water and up out of the boiling sea shot a huge animal, about 60 feet long, writhing and struggling. Shaped like a crocodile, it had four limbs with webbed feet and its long tail tapered to a point. A similar creature was seen from another U-boat in 1918, in the North Sea.

Reports like these indicate that the name 'sea serpent' conceals several different types of beast. The Belgian zoologist Bernard Heuvelmans, after analysing hundreds of sightings, identified seven main varieties of creature. Among them, besides the monstrous

saurian seen from the U-boats, are a 'waterhorse' with a head like a horse or a camel, large eyes, and a mane; a thing like a giant eel; another like a giant otter; and a snake-like creature with many humps on its back, which undulates through the water at high speed and is said to attain a length of as much as 100 feet (30 m).

The type reported more often than any other, however, is a long-necked animal resembling an enormous sea-lion, measuring up to 70 feet (21 m) in length. It has a bulky body, two pairs of flippers, a small head like that of a seal or a dog, small eyes and two small horns or protuberances on its head. One of these, apparently, was seen several times in Falmouth Bay, Cornwall, in 1975 and 1976, and was known locally as Morgawr ('Sea Giant'). One ob-

server described it as 'a sort of prehistoric dinosaur thing, with a long neck the length of a lamp post.'

These strange creatures of the deep are not, of course, 'monsters' in any supernatural sense. If they exist, as they seem to, they are part of the order of nature, and monstrous only in being large and unfamiliar. Popular fancy likes to think of them as 'dinosaur things', huge brutes left over from prehistoric times. Whether there is any truth in this is unknown, but it is not impossible. The belief that no prehistoric species could still exist in the twentieth century has been exploded by the capture, since 1938, of live coelacanths – fish formerly known only from fossil remains and confidently asserted to have been extinct for seventy million years.

ABOVE *The legendary Kraken, seizing a ship in its huge tentacles and dragging it down into the depths: from* The Mysteries of the Ocean *(1870).*

OPPOSITE ABOVE *'Morgawr', the creature seen several times in Falmouth Bay, Cornwall, in 1975 and 1976. This photograph was taken in February 1976 from Rosemullion Head. The animal was described by one person who saw it as 'a sort of prehistoric dinosaur thing with a long neck'.*

OPPOSITE BELOW *The remains of an enormous, mutilated corpse, washed up on the winter tides at St Augustine Beach, Florida, in 1896. The body was 21 feet (6.4 m) across, with octopus-like tentacles as long again.*

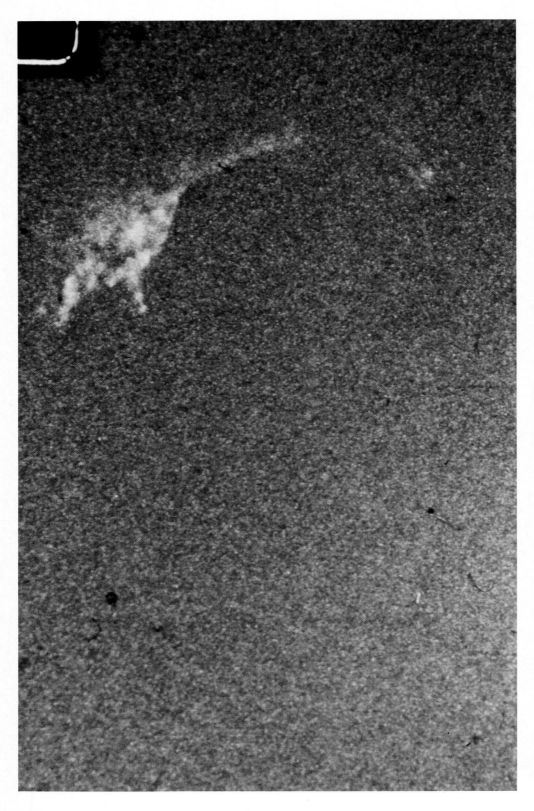

The Loch Ness Monster

Does another creature left over from the age of the dinosaurs live in the black depths of Loch Ness in Scotland? According to one theory, the Loch Ness 'monster' is a plesiosaurus, a massive reptile generally assumed to have died out millions of years ago. Other theories are that the creature – or creatures, as there is presumably more than one –

may be a kind of giant eel or a huge species of seal with a long neck.

St Columba, in the sixth century AD, is the first person recorded to have seen the monster, but there were very few other reports until 1933, when a road along the side of the loch was opened. Thousands of people claim to have seen it since then, but the question of its existence has become blurred in a fog of fakes, hoaxes and silly-season journalism. If it does exist, it apparently has a small head on a long neck, a bulky body, two pairs of flippers, a long tail,

and one or more humps on its back.

The trouble with Loch Ness is that since the 1930s its reputation has positively invited both faked reports and sincere but mistaken reports of sightings. Attempts to find positive proof of the monster's presence, including an underwater search by submarine, have so far failed. Sonar has produced some evidence of large moving objects deep in the loch; hydrophones let down into the water have recorded mysterious clicking noises in the depths; the numerous photographs

of the monster are either disputed or vague. Film shot in 1960 by Tim Dinsdale, a leading Loch Ness investigator, was examined five years later by experts at the Joint Air Reconnaissance Intelligence Unit. They said the film was genuine and showed something large and alive moving across the loch at a speed of a little over ten miles per hour. What it was, unfortunately, the film is too vague to show. In 1975 indistinct underwater photographs were taken of something in the loch. It looked like a plesiosaurus, but many scientists found the photographs unconvincing.

Monsters are said to lurk in many other inland bodies of water, in Russia, Sweden, Iceland, Ireland, Africa, Japan, Australia and New Zealand, and in several lakes in Canada. Again, however, no proof that they are real has yet been found.

The plesiosaurus (above) is assumed to have died out millions of years ago, but could it have survived in the waters of Loch Ness? Despite similarities of shape the underwater photograph taken in 1975 (above left) has failed to convince many scientists.

Bigfoot, Yetis and Wild Men

Other 'monsters' are reported on land. There are rumours that dinosaurs still exist in the Lake Tele area of the Congo: Africans are said to have seen a massive creature with a long neck and a long tail, apparently resembling a brontosaurus.

Equally intriguing are the rumours that some of man's distant ape-like ancestors are still alive. True man was preceded on earth by hominids, man-like creatures or men-apes. Among them was Neanderthal man, who is believed to have died out or been wiped out by true man forty thousand years ago. However, reports have come from remote areas in Russia, China, Tibet, North America and elsewhere of large shaggy animals looking like a cross between man and ape. Shy and rarely seen, they are reputed to attack human beings and cattle on occasion. Descriptions of them suggest the possibility that small groups of hominids have managed to survive and breed in isolated districts, among mountains and forests.

In 1925, in the Pamir Mountains of southern Russia, soldiers shot and killed what may have been a Neanderthal or some other species of hominid. It was a hairy, man-like creature with a sloping forehead, prominent eyebrow ridges, a flat nose and a protruding jaw. There have been numerous other reports from the Caucasus eastwards to Siberia, Mongolia and China of similar 'wild men'. Late in 1980, it was announced that footprints and other evidence found in the mountains of central China suggested the presence of a creature resembling early man.

The most famous and most elusive of the breed is the yeti or Abominable Snowman of the Himalayas. The local people, the Sherpas, who are best placed to know, firmly believe in it and are afraid of it, but their beliefs are dismissed by sceptics as mere superstition. Distant sightings by explorers – there have been very few close encounters – are explained as mistaken observations of langur monkeys or other known animals. Footprints in the snow are the most tangible evidence of the yeti so far. These are also written off, as the tracks of known animals made larger and spuriously mysterious when the imprints begin to melt in the sun. On the other hand, in 1951 the mountaineer Eric Shipton saw and photographed footprints in an unexplored area thirty to forty miles west of Mount Everest. These tracks have not been successfully explained away, and a number of experienced climbers and explorers believe that an unknown beast of some kind exists in the Himalayas.

In the remote mountains and forests of western Canada and the northwestern United States there have been hundreds of reported sightings in the last thirty years of an 'ape-man' known as Bigfoot or by the Indian name of *sasquatch*. He or it is covered with reddish-brown hair, has a backward-sloping forehead and little or no neck, and is said to stand anything from 6 to 10 feet (2 to 3 m) tall. Photographs of Bigfoot have been taken, and footprints discovered, but their genuineness is disputed.

Reports of shaggy 'wild men' go back for centuries and folklore is full of stories of giants – huge, hairy, shambling, primitive, man-like brutes; frightening, anarchic, and often credited with an appetite for human flesh (there is evidence that Neanderthal man was a cannibal). Are these widespread beliefs and tales, however exaggerated, based on a reality – the survival of hominids – and in this sense were there and are there still giants in the earth?

Allowing for hoaxes and mistaken observation, it seems that reliable witnesses have seen things not easy to account for. One explanation is that unknown man-like or ape-like animals

do exist, but if so, it is difficult to understand the absence of convincing evidence – captured specimens, carcasses or bones. Another explanation is that the human mind has a deeply imprinted racial memory of man's predecessors on earth, that it needs them and sometimes calls them into existence, and their footprints with them – the footprints that early hunters may have followed to track and kill their more primitive relatives. What the truth is, no one yet knows. It is the nature of mysteries to remain uncertain and unexplained.

LEFT *Frame from a film of Bigfoot, taken by Roger Patterson on 20 October 1967 at Bluff Creek in northern California. It shows a creature standing about 6 ft 5 in (1.95 m) tall and with a long stride, possibly weighing some 280 lb (127 kg).*

BELOW *Eric Shipton's photograph of a yeti footprint, taken in 1951 in an area to the west of Mount Everest. The prints were on a glacier and led on for several miles. They were considerably deeper than the footprints Shipton and his companion were making.*

BELOW LEFT *Neanderthal man – perhaps he survives in wild, isolated areas.*

Bibliography and Acknowledgments

ASHE, GEOFFREY, *King Arthur's Avalon* (London, 1959)

ASHE, GEOFFREY, *The Ancient Wisdom* (London, 1977)

BALFOUR, MICHAEL, *Stonehenge and its Mysteries* (London, 1979)

BERLITZ, CHARLES, *The Mystery of Atlantis* (New York, 1969; London, 1976)

BERLITZ, CHARLES, *The Bermuda Triangle* (New York, 1974; London, 1975)

BORD, JANET AND COLIN, *Mysterious Britain* (London, 1972)

BOWEN, CHARLES (ed), *Flying Saucer Review*

BROOKESMITH, PETER (ed), *The Unexplained* (London, 1980)

CAVENDISH, RICHARD (ed), *Encyclopedia of the Unexplained* (London and New York, 1974)

CAVENDISH, RICHARD, *King Arthur and the Grail* (London and New York, 1978)

DINSDALE, TIM, *Loch Ness Monster* (second edition, London, 1972)

EDWARDS, I. E. S., *The Pyramids of Egypt* (Harmondsworth and Baltimore, 1961)

FORT, CHARLES, *The Book of the Damned* (London, 1973 reprint)

GALANOPOULOS, A. G., AND BACON, E., *Atlantis* (London, 1969)

HEUVELMANS, BERNARD, *On the Track of Unknown Animals* (London, 1958; New York, 1965)

HEUVELMANS, BERNARD, *In the Wake of the Sea-Serpents* (London and New York, 1968)

HITCHING, FRANCIS, *Earth Magic* (London, 1976)

HITCHING, FRANCIS, *The World Atlas of Mysteries* (London, 1978)

HOYLE, FRED, *On Stonehenge* (London, 1977)

HUGHES, DAVID, *The Star of Bethlehem Mystery* (London, 1979)

KOESTLER, ARTHUR, *The Roots of Coincidence* (London, 1972)

LANCASTER BROWN, PETER, *Megaliths, Myths and Men* (Poole, 1976)

LUCE, J. V., *The End of Atlantis* (London, 1969)

MACKENZIE, ANDREW, *Apparitions and Ghosts* (London, 1971)

MACKIE, EUAN, *The Megalith Builders* (Oxford, 1977)

MATTHEWS, W. H., *Mazes and Labyrinths* (New York, 1970 reprint)

MCEWAN, GRAHAM J., *Sea Serpents, Sailors and Sceptics* (London and Boston, 1978)

MCHARG, J. F., 'A Vision of the Aftermath of the Battle of Nechtansmere' (*Journal of the Society for Psychical Research*, December 1978)

MICHELL, JOHN, *The Flying Saucer Vision* (London, 1969)

MICHELL, JOHN, *The View Over Atlantis* (revised edition, London, 1972)

MICHELL, JOHN, *A Little History of Astro-Archaeology* (London, 1977)

NEAME, ALAN, *The Happening at Lourdes* (London, 1968)

LE POER TRENCH, BRINSLEY, *The Sky People* (London, 1960)

SCREETON, PAUL, *Quicksilver Heritage* (Wellingborough, 1974) (on leys)

SPRAGUE DE CAMP, L., *Lost Continents* (New York, 1970)

STORY, RONALD, *The Space-Gods Revealed* (London, 1977)

STORY, RONALD, *Guardians of the Universe* (London, 1980)

TOMPKINS, PETER, *Secrets of the Great Pyramid* (London and New York, 1973)

TREHARNE, R. F., *The Glastonbury Legends* (London, 1967)

VANDENBERG, PHILIPP, *The Curse of the Pharaohs* (London and New York, 1975)

VON DÄNIKEN, ERICH, *Chariots of the Gods?* (London, 1969; New York, 1971)

WATKINS, ALFRED, *The Old Straight Track* (London, 1970 reprint)

WATSON, LYALL, *Supernature* (London and New York, 1973)

WELFARE, SIMON AND FAIRLEY, JOHN, *Arthur C. Clarke's Mysterious World* (London, 1980)

WILSON, COLIN, *Enigmas and Mysteries* (London, 1976)

WILSON, IAN, *The Turin Shroud* (London and New York, 1978)

WOOD, JOHN EDWIN, *Sun, Moon and Standing Stones* (Oxford, 1978)

The author and publisher would like to thank the following individuals and organizations by whose kind permission the illustrations are reproduced.

AEROFILMS 33 *right*; ASSOCIATED PRESS 56; BARNABY'S PICTURE LIBRARY 65; BBC HULTON PICTURE LIBRARY 9, 24 *bottom*, 46, 48–9; BIRMINGHAM CITY ART GALLERY 40–1; JANET AND COLIN BORD 26 *bottom* (photo Anthony Weir), 36, 38–9; BULLOZ 58; PETER CLAYTON 37 *bottom*; ROBERT ESTALL 4–5, 26 *top*, 27, 30–1, 67 *top*; MARY EVANS PICTURE LIBRARY 50 *vignettes* (photos Society for Psychical Research), 52; FORTEAN PICTURE LIBRARY 1 (photo Anthony Shiels), 57 *top* (photo St Petersburg Times and Evening Independent), 57 *bottom* (photo Larry E. Arnold), 59, 62–3 (photo Anthony Shiels), 66 *top, centre and bottom*, 67 *bottom*, 72, 76–7 (photo Patterson Gimlin); JOHN FROST HISTORICAL NEWSPAPER SERVICE 48; GIRAUDON 50 *main picture*; SONIA HALLIDAY 2–3, 11 *top*; MICHAEL HOLFORD 11 *bottom* (photo Gerry Clyde), 16–17 (photo Ianthe Ruthven), 32, 60–1 (by courtesy of the Trustees of the British Museum); ALAN HUTCHISON 19 *top*, 20; GRAHAM KEEN 37 *top*; KEYSTONE PRESS 53 *left*; KOBAL COLLECTION 13; WILLIAM MACQUITTY 14–15, 16; MANSELL COLLECTION 21, 41, 47 *top and bottom*; TONY MORRISON 34, 35 *top and bottom*, 69; PETER NEWARK'S WESTERN AMERICANA PICTURE LIBRARY 53 *right*; POPPERFOTO 6–7; PRESS ASSOCIATION 54–5; PSYCHIC NEWS 61; REX FEATURES 42, 43; ANN RONAN PICTURE LIBRARY 71, 72–3; ROYAL GEOGRAPHICAL SOCIETY 77 *right* (photo Eric Shipton); SAINT AUGUSTINE HISTORICAL SOCIETY 72; SCALA 8; RONALD SHERIDAN 10, 12, 24 *top*; SPACE FRONTIERS endpapers, 18 *top*, 44–5; SPECTRUM COLOUR LIBRARY 68; SYNDICATION INTERNATIONAL 74 (Academy of Applied Science, Boston, Massachusetts); U.S. GAMES SYSTEMS, NEW YORK 25; WEIDENFELD AND NICOLSON ARCHIVES 51 (photo Kerry Dundas);

Artwork was drawn by Ron Bone (pages 18, 19, 33, 55), Alan Burton (pages 74–5, 77) and Peter North (pages 22–3, 28–9).

The publishers have taken all possible care to trace and acknowledge the ownership of the illustrations. If we have made an incorrect attribution we apologise and will be happy to correct the entry in any future reprint, provided that we receive notification.

Index

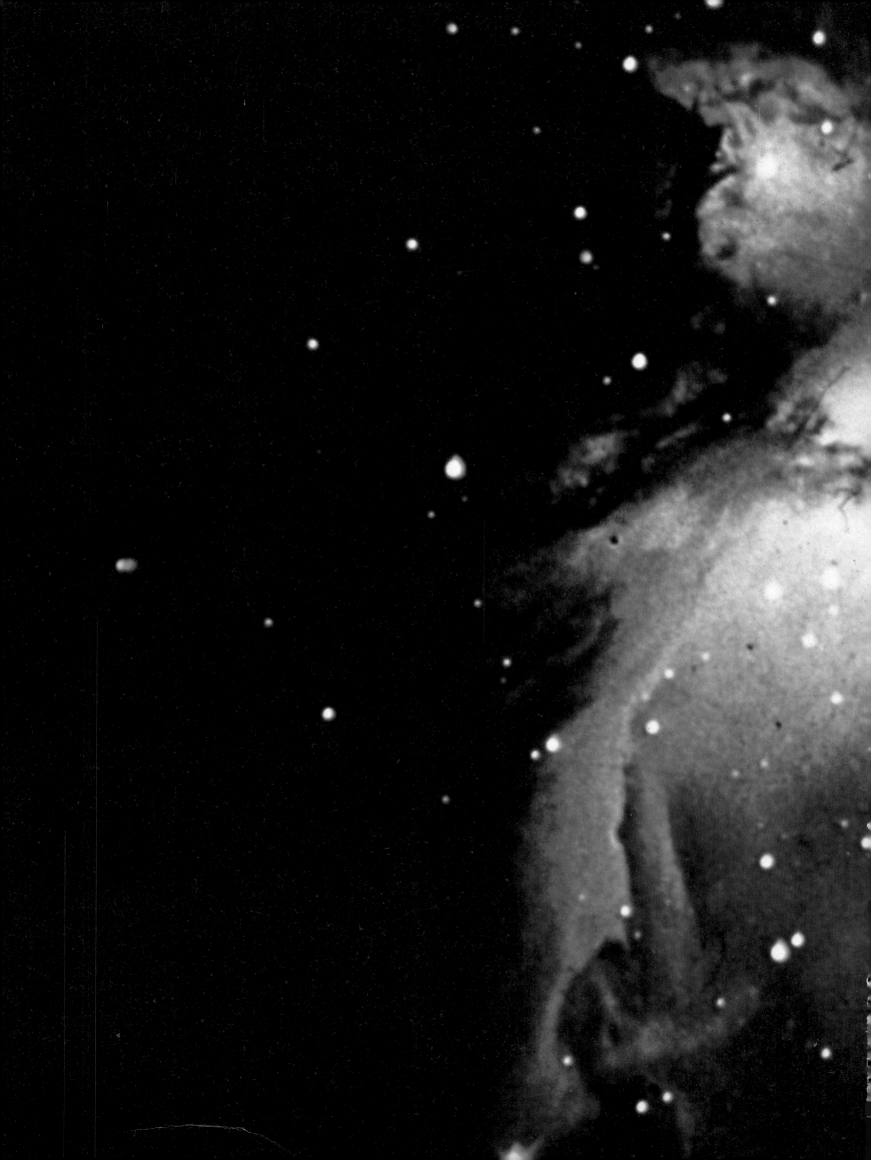